STEAM AWAY THE POUNDS!™

RICHARD SIMMONS

Pascoe Publishing, Inc.
Rocklin, California

© 2006 Salton, Inc., for the interior text and recipes contained herein.
Richard Simmons is a trademark of the Richard Simmons Living Trust.
© 2006 Richard Simmons, Inc. all Rights Reserved

All rights reserved. No part of this book shall be reproduced, stored in a retrieval system, or transmitted by any means, electronic, mechanical, photocopying, recording, or otherwise, without written permission from the publisher. No patent liability is assumed with respect to the use of the information contained herein. Although every precaution has been taken in the preparation of this book, Salton, Inc., The Richard Simmons Living Trust and Pascoe Publishing, Inc. assume no responsibility for errors or omissions. Nor is any liability assumed for damages resulting from the use of the information contained herein.

The nutritional analyses are based on typical serving sizes and optional ingredients have not been included.

Published in the United States of America by

Pascoe Publishing, Inc.
Rocklin, California
www.pascoepublishing.com

Interior Page Design and Layout by Kayla Blanco
Cover Design by Terry Puerzer

Cover and Chapter Opener Photography by Ed Oulette
Steam Heat™ Photography by Robert Weber
Food Photography by Gregory Ross, Ross Studio
Food Styling by Pamela Ross, Ross Studio
Food Photography Assistants: Sarah Turgel and Joshua Steinberg
Food Styling and Infomercial Consulting: Denise Vivaldo, Food Fanatics

Recipe Development and Testing by Robin Taylor-Swatt
Recipe Testing by Connie Neckels
Recipe Nutritional Analyses by Specialized Nutrition Services
Production Coordinator: Debi Bock

ISBN: 1-929862-61-X
ISBN: 978-1-929-862-61-0
06 07 08 09 10

10 9 8 7 6 5 4 3 2 1

Printed in China

TABLE OF CONTENTS

CHAPTER 1: Introduction to Your Steam Heat™ Electronic Steamer — 4

CHAPTER 2: Breakfast Specialties – Quick and Easy Beginnings — 6

CHAPTER 3: Snacks, Appetizers & Salads – Delicious Bites for Any Time of Day — 20

CHAPTER 4: Side Dishes & Vegetables – Flavorful Rice, Potatoes & Vegetables — 40

CHAPTER 5: Entrées – Poultry, Seafood, Pork & Vegetarian Main Dishes — 81

CHAPTER 6: Desserts – Delectable Delights with Fruit, Chocolate & More — 113

CHAPTER 7: Basic Food Charts – Cooking Times & Conversion Charts — 123

INDEX

1 chapter one

Introduction to Your Steam Heat™ Electronic Steamer

Dear Friends,

Some years ago, I envisioned an appliance that would steam a variety of foods to perfection. I wanted to produce a steamer that would allow one to cook all their favorite foods to perfection and be ready at the same time. Impossible, you say? Not so, my friend! Your Steam Heat™ Electronic Steamer is the reality of my vision.

You may ask, "Richard, why would you dream of a steamer like this?" The simple answer is that steaming is one of the most healthful ways to prepare foods with little or no fat. Steaming is easy; it is good for you. Steaming naturally offers the kind of food you want: Fresh, healthful and tasty!

What's unique about your Steam Heat™ Electronic Steamer? First, your steamer contains three horizontal trays that steam foods separately. This prevents food flavors and moisture from intermingling. Other steamers contain two or three vertical trays. The problem with that is they steam from top to bottom. Can you imagine what happens when you steam a salmon fillet in a top tray, corn on the cob in the middle tray and chocolate pudding on the bottom? You get "salmon-corn-chocolate-pudding" for dinner. Count me out!

Your Steam Heat™ Electronic Steamer also contains an electronic timer that can be set separately for each tray. The timer starts each tray at the appropriate time so that all foods are ready at the same time. The result? You sit back and relax while your entire meal is steamed to perfection.

You are going to discover an entirely new world of delicious and delectable flavors in this cookbook. I'm talking about a big world of flavor—global foods, old-fashioned favorites, delightful new food combinations and delectable new creations from my table to yours. Don't be afraid to step out with new herbs, spices and exciting ingredients – I created these recipes to add new interest and flavor to every meal you steam. You are on your way to delicious and healthful meals!

Love,

Richard Simmons

chapter two

Breakfast Specialties
Quick and Easy Beginnings

Super Easy Eggs Benedict
with Hollandaise Sauce

TIMER: Bacon/Eggs – 8 minutes

This recipe has all the flair of Eggs Benedict from your favorite restaurant, but it doesn't have the fat – pure heaven.

nonfat cooking spray
- 4 slices lowfat Canadian bacon (you may use thinly sliced lowfat ham)
- 4 large eggs (you may use 1 cup egg substitute)
- 4 halves whole grain English muffin, toasted

Hollandaise Sauce:
- 3 tablespoons fat-free mayonnaise
- 1 teaspoon Dijon mustard
- 2 teaspoons fresh lemon juice

pinch white pepper
fresh minced parsley for garnish

Lightly coat the Cooking Bowl with the cooking spray. Place the Canadian bacon slices on the bottom of the bowl. Carefully crack the eggs over the bacon, without breaking the yolks. Place in the Center Steamer Bowl and set the timer for 8 minutes, start the steamer and steam until the eggs are set to your preference. Meanwhile, whisk together the *Hollandaise Sauce* ingredients.

When the timer goes off, carefully remove the Cooking Bowl and place one English muffin half on each of four individual plates. Using a large serving spoon, scoop out the four eggs and bacon and place equally on the four muffins. Spoon the *Hollandaise Sauce* equally over the eggs. Garnish with parsley and serve.

Serves 4.

CALORIES 209, TOTAL FAT 8G, SATURATED FAT 2G, % CALORIES FROM FAT 33, CARBOHYDRATES 17G, PROTEIN 19G, CHOLESTEROL 237MG, SODIUM 853MG

Strawberries & Cream Porridge

TIMER: Porridge–10 minutes

Goldilocks kept trying to find the bowl of porridge that was just right – I think this is it!

- ½ cup polenta or brown rice farina
- 1 cup nonfat milk
- ½ cup strawberries, sliced
- 2 tablespoons nonfat sour cream
- 2 teaspoons honey

Place the polenta (or farina) and milk in the Cooking Bowl, mixing well to combine. Place in the Center Steamer Bowl and set the timer for 10 minutes. Start the steamer.

When the timer goes off, carefully remove the Cooking Bowl from the steamer and spoon into two individual bowls. Layer the strawberry slices, sour cream and honey over the porridge and serve.

Serves 2.

CALORIES 250, TOTAL FAT 3G, SATURATED FAT <1G, % CALORIES FROM FAT 10, CARBOHYDRATES 46G, PROTEIN 10G, CHOLESTEROL 10MG, SODIUM 364MG

Breakfast Specialties 9

Asparagus & Ricotta Frittata
(Say This Three Times Fast...)

TIMER: Frittata–10 minutes, Asparagus–7 minutes

What is a "frittata?" A frittata is an open-faced dish that is cooked in an open pan. Originally from Italy, the delicate egg dish typically contains vegetables or other breakfast-type ingredients.

- 4 spears fresh asparagus, woody ends trimmed
- 2 large eggs, beaten (you may use ½ cup egg substitute)
- ¼ cup fat-free ricotta cheese
- 1 teaspoon fresh thyme leaves, chopped
- pinch kosher salt
- ¼ teaspoon freshly ground black pepper

Place the asparagus, eggs, cheese, thyme, salt and pepper into the Cooking Bowl. Place the Cooking Bowl in the Center Steamer Bowl and set the timer for 10 minutes. Start the steamer and steam until the eggs are set to your preference. When done, carefully remove the frittata from the steamer. Spoon the frittata onto two individual plates and serve.

Serves 2.

CALORIES 107, TOTAL FAT 5G, SATURATED FAT 2G, % CALORIES FROM FAT 44, CARBOHYDRATES 4G, PROTEIN 11G, CHOLESTEROL 215MG, SODIUM 242MG

Chicken & Black Bean Breakfast Burritos

TIMER: Burrito—10 minutes, Tortilla—5 minutes

As deep-dish pizza is to Chicago, Mexican-American burritos are to San Francisco. In the early 1960s chefs in the Mission district began experimenting with burritos, packing all kinds of fun ingredients into new creations. My breakfast burrito carries on the creative tradition in grand style – enjoy!

- nonfat cooking spray
- 4 large eggs, beaten (you may use 1 cup egg substitute)
- 4 slices lowfat smoked chicken or turkey, diced (you may use steamed, cooked chicken or turkey, if desired)
- 1/3 cup canned black beans, drained
- 2 Roma tomatoes, seeded and diced
- 3 green onions, thinly sliced
- 8 dashes prepared hot sauce
- 4 8-inch lowfat whole wheat tortillas
- 1/4 cup nonfat sour cream
- 1/3 cup lowfat Monterey Jack cheese

Lightly coat the Cooking Bowl with cooking spray. Place the eggs, chicken, black beans, tomatoes, green onions and hot sauce in the bowl and stir to combine. Place the bowl in the Center Steamer Bowl and set the timer for 10 minutes. Wrap the tortillas in aluminum foil and place in both Side Steamer Bowls. Set the timer for 5 minutes.

Start the steamer. When done, remove the burrito mixture and tortillas from the steamer. Place the eggs equally in each of the four tortillas and add a dollop of sour cream on top of the eggs. Add the cheese and add more hot sauce, if desired. Fold the bottom and sides of each tortilla to form an envelope and serve.

Makes 4 breakfast burritos.

CALORIES 243, TOTAL FAT 8G, SATURATED FAT 3G, % CALORIES FROM FAT 30, CARBOHYDRATES 25G, PROTEIN 17G, CHOLESTEROL 230MG, SODIUM 642MG

Run-to-the-Office Breakfast Pita

TIMER: Pita—10 minutes

For those days when you're late, late, late and you can't sit down and wait.

- 1 slice lowfat cooked turkey, diced
- 1 large egg, beaten (you may use ¼ cup egg substitute)
- 1 ounce lowfat cheddar cheese, shredded
- 1 green onion, sliced
- pinch freshly ground black pepper
- nonfat cooking spray
- one-half whole wheat pita bread pocket

Place the diced turkey, beaten egg, cheese, green onion and pepper in a small mixing bowl and beat to combine. Lightly coat the Cooking Bowl with cooking spray. Pour the turkey-egg mixture into the bowl. Place in the Center Steamer Bowl and set the timer for 10 minutes.

Start the steamer and steam until the egg is set to your preference. When the timer goes off, carefully remove the scrambled egg from the steamer. Spoon into the pita pocket and wrap the pita in a napkin. Grab your briefcase and go.

Makes 1 breakfast pita.

CALORIES 281, TOTAL FAT 8G, SATURATED FAT 3G, % CALORIES FROM FAT 25, CARBOHYDRATES 29G, PROTEIN 24G, CHOLESTEROL 219MG, SODIUM 506MG

Noteworthy Northwest Scramble

TIMER: Scramble—10 minutes

The Pacific Northwest is known for salmon – fresh, smoked, barbecued – any way they can make it! What I like about this recipe is that the smoked salmon delivers a great burst of flavor without overwhelming the eggs, tomatoes and green onions. Velvety cream cheese adds the "ooh-ah" factor!

    nonfat cooking spray
 3 ounces smoked salmon, minced
 4 large eggs, beaten (you may use 1 cup egg substitute)
 2 Roma tomatoes, seeded and diced
 2 green onions, thinly sliced
 4 tablespoons fat-free cream cheese

Lightly coat the Cooking Bowl with the cooking spray. Place the smoked salmon, beaten eggs, tomatoes and green onions in the Cooking Bowl and blend with a large spoon to combine. Place in the Center Steamer Bowl and set the timer for 10 minutes.

Start the steamer and steam until the eggs are set to your preference. When the timer goes off, carefully remove the egg scramble from the steamer. Spoon the eggs equally onto four individual plates and add a spoonful of cream cheese on top of each serving.

Serves 4.

CALORIES 136, TOTAL FAT 6G, SATURATED FAT 2G, % CALORIES FROM FAT 43, CARBOHYDRATES 5G, PROTEIN 15G, CHOLESTEROL 219MG, SODIUM 424MG

Breakfast Specialties 13

Southwestern Style Eggs
with Parsley Buttered Red Potatoes

TIMER: Potatoes–45 minutes, Eggs–10 minutes

Wake up those taste buds and teach them to salsa! To create a fancy look, prepare the eggs in a small tart or mini springform pan.

- 6 small red potatoes, rinsed and cut into quarters
- 2 tablespoons lowfat butter-flavored spread
- ¼ cup fresh parsley, chopped, divided
- nonfat cooking spray
- 4 eggs, beaten (you may use 1 cup egg substitute)
- ½ cup canned black beans, drained
- ½ cup roasted red peppers, diced
- ½ cup fresh corn kernels (you may use frozen, thawed corn)
- 4 ounces lowfat Monterey Jack cheese, shredded
- ½ teaspoon chili powder

Place the potatoes in the Side Steamer Bowl and set the timer for 45 minutes. Lightly coat the Cooking Bowl with cooking spray. Place the eggs, black beans, red peppers, corn, cheese and 2 tablespoons of the parsley in the bowl. Add the chili powder and blend with a large spoon to combine. Place in the Center Steamer Bowl and set the timer for 10 minutes.

Start the steamer. When the timer goes off, carefully remove the eggs and divide equally onto four individual plates. Remove the potatoes and coat them evenly with the lowfat spread. Garnish the potatoes with the remaining parsley and add to the four plates.

Serves 4.

CALORIES 281, TOTAL FAT 13G, SATURATED FAT 6G, % CALORIES FROM FAT 38, CARBOHYDRATES 24G, PROTEIN 21G, CHOLESTEROL 233MG, SODIUM 503MG

Banana & Walnut Oatmeal

TIMER: Oatmeal—10 minutes

If you love the aroma of fresh banana bread baking in the kitchen, this cereal will be your new favorite breakfast food.

- 1 cup quick cooking oats
- 1 cup nonfat milk
- ½ cup banana, thinly sliced
- 2 teaspoons honey
- 1 teaspoon walnuts, finely chopped

Place the oats, milk and banana in the Cooking Bowl, mixing well to combine. Place in the Center Steamer Bowl and set the timer for 10 minutes. Start the steamer.

When the timer goes off, carefully remove the Cooking Bowl from the steamer and spoon the oatmeal into two individual bowls. Add the honey and walnuts equally to each bowl of oatmeal and serve.

Serves 2.

CALORIES 495, TOTAL FAT 11G, SATURATED FAT 2G, % CALORIES FROM FAT 19, CARBOHYDRATES 81G, PROTEIN 21G, CHOLESTEROL 7MG, SODIUM 91MG

Breakfast Specialties 15

Easy Huevos Rancheros
(or "Easy Huevos Apartments" if You Don't Live on a Ranch)

TIMER: Eggs–8 minutes, Tortillas–5 minutes

No matter where you live, you'll love the zesty combination of these eggs. You can find cotija cheese in the deli of your grocery store or substitute feta cheese if you prefer.

   nonfat cooking spray
4 large eggs (you may use 1 cup egg subsitute)
½ cup fat-free refried beans
4 6-inch lowfat tortillas (you may use whole wheat, if desired)
½ cup mild, smooth tomato salsa
¼ cup lowfat cotija cheese

Lightly coat the Cooking Bowl with cooking spray. Carefully crack the eggs and place in the bowl, without breaking the yolks. Place in the Center Steamer Bowl and set the timer for 8 minutes. Check the eggs for your preference and continue steaming if necessary. Spread each tortilla with the refried beans. Wrap each tortilla in a square of aluminum foil. Place two in each of the two Side Steamer Bowls and set the timer for 5 minutes. Start the steamer.

When the timer goes off, carefully remove the eggs and let stand. Remove the tortillas and slide each out of the foil onto 2 individual plates. Gently remove the cooked eggs from the Cooking Bowl and spoon equally onto the tortillas. Top each with the tomato salsa and lowfat cheese and serve.

Serves 4.

CALORIES 243, TOTAL FAT 6G, SATURATED FAT 2G, % CALORIES FROM FAT 21, CARBOHYDRATES 35G, PROTEIN 14G, CHOLESTEROL 213MG, SODIUM 788MG

Cinnamon-Spiced Apples
with Blueberries and Yogurt

TIMER: Apple Mixture—10 minutes

Is this breakfast or dessert? This parfait is made of layers of good-for-you apples, blueberries and yogurt, topped with a sprinkling of crunchy wheat germ. YUM!

- 1 medium Fuji apple, peeled and sliced
- 1 teaspoon fresh lemon juice
- ½ teaspoon ground cinnamon
- 1 tablespoon brown sugar, packed
- 1 cup fresh blueberries, rinsed and drained
- 1 cup nonfat vanilla yogurt
- 2 tablespoons toasted wheat germ

Place the apple slices, lemon juice, cinnamon and brown sugar in the Cooking Bowl and mix to combine. Place in the Center Steamer Bowl and set the timer for 10 minutes. Start the steamer and steam until the apple slices are warm throughout. When done, carefully remove the apple slices from the steamer.

Combine the apple slices and spices with the blueberries and toss lightly. Using two parfait glasses, spoon the mixed fruit equally into each glass. Top with a layer of the yogurt and sprinkle the toasted wheat germ over each serving.

Serves 2.

CALORIES 254, TOTAL FAT 1G, SATURATED FAT <1G, % CALORIES FROM FAT 3, CARBOHYDRATES 50G, PROTEIN 13G, CHOLESTEROL 10MG, SODIUM 159MG

Breakfast Specialties

Gingered Peaches
with Cottage Cheese & Granola

TIMER: Gingered Peaches—8 minutes

Start with sweet, ripe peaches and infuse them with the flavor of fresh ginger. The cool cottage cheese and granola add delicious texture to the sweet and spicy peaches.

- 2 large peaches, peeled and sliced
- 1 teaspoon fresh lemon juice
- 1 teaspoon ground cinnamon
- 1 tablespoon dark brown sugar, packed
- ¼ teaspoon fresh ginger, minced
- 1 teaspoon water
- 1 cup nonfat small-curd cottage cheese
- ½ cup lowfat crunchy granola mix

Place the peaches, lemon juice, cinnamon and brown sugar in the Cooking Bowl and stir to combine. Place the minced fresh ginger and water in the Flavor Tray. Place the peach mixture in the Center Steamer Bowl, set the timer for 8 minutes and start the steamer.

When the timer goes off, carefully remove the peaches from the steamer. To serve, spoon the spiced peach slices into two individual bowls. Cover each with the nonfat cottage cheese and top with the granola.

Serves 2.

CALORIES 304, TOTAL FAT 1G, SATURATED FAT <1G, % CALORIES FROM FAT 4, CARBOHYDRATES 41G, PROTEIN 30G, CHOLESTEROL 10MG, SODIUM 840MG

Orange-Spiced Pears
with Almond Ricotta

TIMER: Pears—8 minutes

You may normally use ricotta cheese in lasagna or other Italian dishes, but this naturally lowfat cheese is delightfully smooth and rich for breakfast, too!

- 1 large Bosc or Anjou pear, peeled and sliced
- 1 teaspoon fresh orange juice
- ½ teaspoon fresh orange zest
- ¼ teaspoon ground nutmeg
- ¼ teaspoon ground cloves
- 2 cups fat-free ricotta cheese
- 1 tablespoon honey
- ⅛ teaspoon almond extract
- 1 tablespoon almonds, sliced

Place the pear, orange juice, orange zest, nutmeg, and cloves in the Cooking Bowl. Mix with a spoon to lightly combine. Place the pear mixture in the Center Steamer Bowl, set the timer for 8 minutes and start the steamer.

In a small bowl, combine the ricotta cheese with the honey and almond extract. When the timer goes off, carefully remove the pears from the steamer. Top the steamed pears with the sweetened ricotta cheese. Spoon the pears into two individual bowls and garnish each serving with the almonds. Serve at once.

Serves 2.

CALORIES 304, TOTAL FAT 4G, SATURATED FAT 1G, % CALORIES FROM FAT 11, CARBOHYDRATES 35G, PROTEIN 35G, CHOLESTEROL 23MG, SODIUM 4898MG

Mediterranean Tofu & Tomatoes

TIMER: Tofu–10 minutes, Pita Bread–5 minutes

If you've been avoiding tofu because you are unsure of how it will taste, this is the perfect "starter" recipe for you. Silken tofu has a creamy texture and adds a nice protein boost to your dishes.

- 1 cup silken tofu, chopped
- 2 Roma tomatos, seeded and diced
- ¼ cup red onion, minced
- ¼ cup kalamata olives, seeded and chopped
- ¾ cup fat-free feta cheese, crumbled
- 2 teaspoons fresh oregano leaves, chopped
- 1 round pita bread, cut in half and split to form pockets

Place all of the ingredients except the pita bread in the Cooking Bowl and toss lightly to combine. Place in the Center Steamer Bowl and set the timer for 10 minutes. Wrap the pita bread in aluminum foil and place in the Side Steamer Bowl.

Set the timer for 5 minutes. Start the steamer. When done, carefully remove the tofu and vegetables and the pita bread. Spoon the tofu mixture into each half of the pita bread and serve.

Serves 2.

CALORIES 264, TOTAL FAT 7G, SATURATED FAT <1G, % CALORIES FROM FAT 24, CARBOHYDRATES 29G, PROTEIN 20G, CHOLESTEROL 4MG, SODIUM 708MG

3 chapter three

Snacks, Appetizers & Salads
Delicious Bites for Any Time of Day

Snacks, Appetizers & Salads

Steamed Edamame

TIMER: Edamame–5 minutes

Edamame (Ed-uh-mă-may) are fresh soybean pods that have long been utilized as appetizers in Japanese meals. They are fun to eat as snacks or appetizers.

- 1 pound fresh or frozen, thawed edamame
- ¼ teaspoon kosher salt

Place the edamame in the Center Steamer Bowl and set the timer for 5 minutes. Start the steamer. When the timer goes off, carefully remove the edamame from the steamer.

Immediately sprinkle with salt and toss lightly. Serve warm or cool. To eat, remove the beans from the pods and discard the pods.

Serves 4.

CALORIES 160, TOTAL FAT 7G, SATURATED FAT <1G, % CALORIES FROM FAT 37, CARBOHYDRATES 12G, PROTEIN 13G, CHOLESTEROL 0MG, SODIUM 131MG

Turkey Potstickers

TIMER: Potstickers—28 minutes

Steamed potstickers are like little best friends...serve with Asian Dipping Sauce.

- ½ pound ground lean turkey
- 2 green onions, sliced
- 1 clove garlic, minced
- 2 teaspoons fresh ginger, grated
- 2 tablespoons water chestnuts, finely chopped
- 2 tablespoons egg substitute
- 20 round potsticker wrappers

Asian Dipping Sauce Ingredients:
- ¼ cup low-sodium soy sauce
- 1 tablespoon spicy hot or Dijon mustard
- ½ teaspoon crushed red pepper flakes

Combine the turkey, onions, garlic, ginger, water chestnuts and egg substitute in a mixing bowl. Place one teaspoon of the mixture in the center of each potsticker wrapper. Fold the round wrapper in half, using water to seal the wrapper, to form a half-moon shape. Crimp the seal with the tines of a fork. Place the potstickers in the Center Steamer Bowl and set the timer for 28 minutes. Start the steamer.

Combine the ingredients for the dipping sauce in a small bowl and whisk until blended. When the potstickers are done, check one with the tip of a knife. The turkey should be cooked all the way through with no pink remaining. Transfer the potstickers to a serving platter and serve while warm with the *Asian Dipping Sauce*.

Serves 10.

 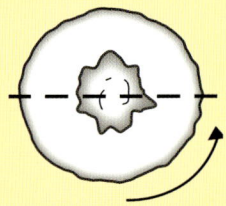 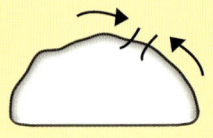 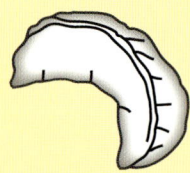

CALORIES 82, TOTAL FAT <1G, SATURATED FAT <1G, % CALORIES FROM FAT 7, CARBOHYDRATES 11G, PROTEIN 8G, CHOLESTEROL 12MG, SODIUM 361MG

Southwest Bean Dip
with Crisp Red Pepper Strips

TIMER: Bean Dip–30 minutes, Red pepper strips–5 minutes

The hidden beauty of this dip and "chip" combination is in the crisp red pepper strips. They are slightly sweet – you won't miss those tortilla chips!

1	cup fat-free vegetarian refried beans
¼	cup prepared spicy tomato salsa
¼	cup lowfat cheddar cheese, shredded
4	large red bell peppers, cored, seeded and sliced into 1-inch strips
1	green onion, thinly sliced

Combine the beans, salsa and cheddar cheese in the Cooking Bowl, mixing to blend. Place in the Center Steamer Bowl and set the timer for 30 minutes. Place the pepper strips in a Side Steamer Bowl and set the timer for 5 minutes. Start the steamer.

When the timer goes off, remove the dip and garnish with the green onions. Remove the red pepper strips and serve with the dip in place of chips.

Serves 8.

CALORIES 62, TOTAL FAT <1G, SATURATED FAT <1G, % CALORIES FROM FAT 11, CARBOHYDRATES 13G, PROTEIN 4G, CHOLESTEROL <1MG, SODIUM 213MG

Bagna Cauda with Vegetables

TIMER: Bagna Cauda–30 minutes, Carrots–7 minutes, Broccoli–5 minutes

If you know what "bagna cauda" is, give yourself five points. If you don't know, but are adventurous enough to try it, give yourself twenty points! This is a popular French dipping sauce paired with steamed vegetables.

- 4 cloves garlic, minced
- 2 ounces anchovies, rinsed and minced
- 2 tablespoons lowfat, butter-flavored spread
- 1 cup low-sodium chicken or vegetable broth
- 2 cups fresh broccoli, cleaned and cut into small florets
- 2 cups baby carrots, rinsed and dried

Combine the garlic, anchovies, butter-flavored spread and broth in the Cooking Bowl. Place in the Center Steamer Bowl and set the timer for 30 minutes. Place the broccoli florets in a Side Steamer Bowl and set the timer for 5 minutes. Place the baby carrots in the other Side Steamer Bowl and set the timer for 7 minutes.

Start the steamer. When the timer goes off, remove the sauce and vegetables from the steamer. To serve, place the warmed dipping sauce in the middle of a platter and surround it with the steamed vegetables. Dip the vegetables in the delicious sauce.

Serves 8.

CALORIES 40, TOTAL FAT 1G, SATURATED FAT <1G, % CALORIES FROM FAT 30, CARBOHYDRATES 5G, PROTEIN 3G, CHOLESTEROL 5MG, SODIUM 250MG

Snacks, Appetizers & Salads 25

Sour Cream Deviled Eggs

TIMER: Eggs–18 minutes

Your Steam Heat™ Electronic Steamer prepares hard-cooked eggs in a snap! Eggs are steamed perfectly every time, without pans of boiling water. A nice added feature is that the eggs easily stand up in the steamer and you can cook over a dozen at a time.

- 12 large eggs
- ¼ cup lowfat mayonnaise
- ¼ cup nonfat sour cream
- 1 teaspoon Dijon mustard
- ¼ teaspoon salt
- ½ teaspoon freshly ground black pepper
- 3 green onions, divided
- ground paprika, for garnish

Place the eggs upright in the Center or Side Steamer Bowls. Steam for 18 minutes. Remove one egg and peel. If the egg is hard-cooked, remove the remaining eggs. If not, continue steaming for 2 minutes. When done, remove the eggs from the steamer and immerse in a bowl of cold water for 5 minutes. This stops the cooking action and aids in removing the peel. Peel the eggs, cut in half length-wise and arrange the cooked egg whites on a serving plate.

Place the yolks in a medium bowl and mash with a fork. Add the mayonnaise, sour cream, mustard, salt, pepper and 2 minced green onions. Mix together until smooth. Spoon the filling into the egg halves and sprinkle each with a bit of the remaining green onion. Garnish the eggs with paprika. Serve immediately or chill in the refrigerator until serving.

Serves 12 as an appetizer.

CALORIES 103, TOTAL FAT 7G, SATURATED FAT 4G, % CALORIES FROM FAT 46, CARBOHYDRATES 3G, PROTEIN 8G, CHOLESTEROL 213MG, SODIUM 123MG

Chilled Shrimp
with Cocktail Sauce

TIMER: Shrimp–8 minutes

Simple, elegant and a crowd-pleaser every time, this appetizer of chilled shrimp is easy to prepare and even easier to serve.

- 3 tablespoons fresh lemon juice, divided
- ¾ pound large shrimp, shelled, deveined, tails on
- 1 tablespoon fresh Italian flat leaf parsley, finely chopped
- ½ cup prepared lowfat cocktail sauce

Place 2 tablespoons of lemon juice in the Flavor Tray. Place the shrimp in the Center Steamer Bowl and set the timer for 8 minutes. Start the steamer. Check the shrimp and continue steaming, if necessary, until all of the shrimp are pink.

Remove and place the shrimp in a serving bowl or platter. Drizzle with the remaining lemon juice and garnish with the parsley. Place in the refrigerator to chill for at least 30 minutes. Serve the shrimp over ice. Serve the cocktail sauce for dipping on the side.

Serves 6.

CALORIES 82, TOTAL FAT <1G, SATURATED FAT <1G, % CALORIES FROM FAT 11, CARBOHYDRATES 6G, PROTEIN 12G, CHOLESTEROL 86MG, SODIUM 311MG

Chinese Shrimp & Water Chestnut Dumplings

TIMER: Potstickers—15 minutes

Most dumplings and potstickers served in Chinese restaurants are fried after they are steamed or boiled. In contrast, mine are really low in fat and high in flavor. Serve with the Asian Dipping Sauce *on page 22.*

- 6 ounces raw shrimp, finely chopped
- 2 tablespoons canned bamboo shoots, finely chopped
- 2 tablespoons canned water chestnuts, finely chopped
- 1 green onion, finely chopped
- ¼ teaspoon toasted sesame oil
- 12 round potsticker wrappers

Combine the shrimp, bamboo shoots, water chestnuts, green onion and sesame oil in a medium bowl. Place about 2 teaspoons of the filling in the center of each potsticker wrapper. Fold the wrapper in half, using water to seal the wrapper, to form a half-moon. See instructions on page 22.

Crimp the seal with your fingers or with the tines of a fork. Place the potstickers in the Center Steamer Bowl and set the timer for 15 minutes. Start the steamer. When the timer goes off, carefully remove from the steamer and place on a serving platter.

Serves 6.

CALORIES 83, TOTAL FAT <1G, SATURATED FAT <1G, % CALORIES FROM FAT 11, CARBOHYDRATES 11G, PROTEIN 7G, CHOLESTEROL 45MG, SODIUM 135MG

Vegetable Cream Cheese Pinwheels

TIMER: Eggplant–12 minutes, Onion/peppers–15 minutes, Tortillas–5 minutes

Without a doubt, these will become the hit of the party! Find some of those cool picks with gold or silver twirls so that these will look really spiffy on the platter.

- 1 large eggplant, chopped
- 10 button mushrooms, rinsed and cleaned
- 2 cloves garlic, minced, divided
- 1 medium yellow onion, peeled and chopped
- 2 red bell peppers, seeded and chopped
- 8 8-inch lowfat flour tortillas
- 1 8 ounce package nonfat cream cheese, softened
- ½ cup nonfat plain yogurt
- 1 teaspoon no-sodium garlic seasoning
- 1 tablespoon fresh Italian flat leaf parsley, finely chopped
- 1 tablespoon fresh thyme leaves, finely chopped
- 1 tablespoon fresh mint leaves, finely chopped

Combine the eggplant, mushrooms and one-half of the garlic in the Center Steamer Bowl. Set the timer for 12 minutes. Combine the onion, peppers and the remaining garlic in a Side Steamer Bowl. Set the timer for 15 minutes. Wrap the tortillas in aluminum foil, place in a Side Steamer Bowl and set the timer for 5 minutes. Start the steamer. Combine the cream cheese, yogurt, garlic seasoning, parsley, thyme and mint and blend until smooth. When the timer goes off, remove the vegetables and cool slightly.

Chop the vegetables into small pieces and combine in a medium bowl. Remove any excess moisture and set aside. Remove the tortillas and spread the cream cheese mixture over each. Place equal portions of the vegetables over the cream cheese and roll the tortillas tightly. Wrap the rolls tightly in plastic wrap and refrigerate for up to 2 hours. Cut the rolled tortillas into slices 1-inch apart to form pinwheels. Secure each pinwheel with a pick and chill until ready to serve.

Serves 12.

CALORIES 90, TOTAL FAT <1G, SATURATED FAT <1G, % CALORIES FROM FAT 2, CARBOHYDRATES 16G, PROTEIN 6G, CHOLESTEROL 4MG, SODIUM 223MG

Vineyard Chicken Salad

TIMER: Chicken—18 minutes

This salad is impressive enough for your most important guests and easy enough to serve to your kids.

- 1 teaspoon Dijon mustard
- 1 boneless, skinless chicken breast
- 1 teaspoon dried tarragon leaves, crushed
- ¼ teaspoon freshly ground black pepper
- ½ cup red or green seedless grapes, halved
- 1 tablespoon pecans, chopped
- 2 stalks celery, sliced
- 2 cups baby arugula leaves or mixed greens

Vinaigrette Ingredients:
- 1 teaspoon water
- 1 teaspoon extra-virgin olive oil
- 1 teaspoon red wine vinegar
- ½ teaspoon Dijon mustard
- ¼ teaspoon sugar substitute
- ¼ teaspoon kosher salt
- ¼ teaspoon freshly ground black pepper

Spread the Dijon mustard over the chicken breast until it is lightly coated. Dust the tarragon and black pepper over the top of the mustard. Place the chicken breast in the Center or Side Steamer Bowl and set the timer for 18 minutes. Start the steamer. When done, remove the chicken and check with the tip of a knife. Continue steaming if necessary, until no pink remains and the internal temperature of the chicken reaches 180°F. Cool slightly.

Chop the cooled chicken into bite-sized pieces and place in a salad bowl. Toss with the grapes, pecans and celery. In a small mixing bowl, whisk together all of the vinaigrette ingredients. Drizzle the vinaigrette over the chicken salad and toss lightly again until the dressing is coated throughout. To serve, evenly divide the arugula or mixed greens on two plates and spoon the chicken salad over the greens.

Serves 2.

CALORIES 172, TOTAL FAT 6G, SATURATED FAT <1G, % CALORIES FROM FAT 32, CARBOHYDRATES 14G, PROTEIN 13G, CHOLESTEROL 21MG, SODIUM 1005MG

Salad Niçoise

TIMER: Egg–18 minutes, Green Beans–12 minutes, Ahi Tuna–3 minutes

Don't let the fancy name intimidate you – this salad is easy to prepare and luscious to eat! Garnish with assorted baby tomatoes and herbs. You can also steam additional eggs in the steamer for later uses, such as for sandwiches and salads.

- 1 large egg
- 1 pound fresh ahi tuna steak
- 1 pound fresh green beans, trimmed
- 2 Roma tomatoes, sliced
- 2 tablespoons kalamata olives, chopped
- 2 teaspoons capers
- ½ cup red onion, thinly sliced
- 4 cups fresh mixed salad greens of your choice

Vinaigrette Ingredients:
- 2 teaspoons water
- 2 teaspoons extra-virgin olive oil
- 2 teaspoons white wine vinegar
- 1 teaspoon Dijon mustard
- 1 teaspoon dried thyme
- ½ teaspoon kosher salt
- ½ teaspoon freshly ground black pepper

Place the egg upright in a small dimple in the Side Steamer Bowl. Set the timer for 18 minutes. Place the tuna in the Cooking Bowl in the Center Steamer Bowl and set the timer for 3 minutes. Place the green beans in the remaining Side Steamer Bowl and set the timer for 12 minutes. Start the steamer. When the timer goes off, the tuna will be rare. Continue steaming, if desired. Remove the egg, tuna and green beans and cool. Peel the egg and slice.

Cut the tuna into chunks or slices. Slice each green bean in half widthwise. Place the vinaigrette ingredients in a small bowl and whisk to combine. Set aside. On a medium platter, place the salad greens. Arrange the egg slices, tuna chunks, green beans, sliced tomatoes and olives on top of the greens. Top with the capers and sliced red onion. Drizzle with the vinaigrette and serve.

Serves 3.

CALORIES 366, TOTAL FAT 7G, SATURATED FAT <1G, % CALORIES FROM FAT 19, CARBOHYDRATES 24G, PROTEIN 43G, CHOLESTEROL 139MG, SODIUM 527MG

California Turkey Cobb Salad

TIMER: Egg–18 minutes, Turkey–16 minutes

What puts the "California" in this cobb salad? The avocado, of course! You can steam additional eggs for later uses, such as for sandwiches and salads.

- 1 large egg
- 1 6 ounce turkey cutlet
- 3 cups assorted salad greens, rinsed and chilled
- 1 slice low-sodium turkey bacon, cooked and chopped
- ½ cup cherry or grape tomatoes
- ¼ medium ripe Haas avocado, thinly sliced
- ¼ cup carrot, peeled and grated
- 1 tablespoon bleu cheese, crumbled

Dressing Ingredients:
- ½ cup nonfat mayonnaise
- 1 tablespoon fresh lemon juice
- 1 tablespoon water
- 1 teaspoon freshly ground black pepper

Place the large egg in a Side Steamer Bowl and set the timer for 18 minutes. Place the turkey cutlet in the Center Steamer Bowl and set the timer for 16 minutes. Start the steamer. When the timer goes off, check the turkey with the tip of a knife and continue steaming if necessary, until no pink remains and the internal temperature of the turkey reaches 180°F. Remove the egg and turkey from the Steamer Bowls and cool.

Peel the egg and slice. Cut the cooled turkey cutlet into bite-sized pieces. On a serving platter, arrange the salad greens. Layer the egg slices, turkey pieces, bacon, tomatoes, avocado and grated carrot on top. Whisk together in a small bowl the dressing ingredients and drizzle over the salad. Garnish with the bleu cheese and serve.

Serves 3.

CALORIES 207, TOTAL FAT 7G, SATURATED FAT 2G, % CALORIES FROM FAT 32, CARBOHYDRATES 15G, PROTEIN 21G, CHOLESTEROL 76MG, SODIUM 513MG

Chicken Curry Salad

TIMER: Chicken—18 minutes

The best part of this salad is the crunch factor! Almonds, apples, raisins and celery all tossed with a lemony dressing – what's not to like here?

- 2 boneless, skinless chicken breasts
- 1 medium Granny Smith apple, chopped
- ¼ cup golden raisins
- 2 stalks celery, chopped
- 1 tablespoon almonds, toasted
- 1 tablespoon fresh Italian flat-leaf parsley, chopped
- 6 large lettuce leaves, for garnish

Dressing Ingredients:
- ¼ cup nonfat plain yogurt
- ¼ cup nonfat mayonnaise
- 2 teaspoons curry powder
- 1 teaspoon fresh lemon juice
- 1 teaspoon mango chutney
- ¼ teaspoon dried mint

Place the chicken in the Center Steamer Bowl and set the timer for 18 minutes. When the timer goes off, remove the chicken and check with the tip of a knife. Continue steaming if necessary, until no pink remains and the internal temperature of the chicken reaches 180°F. Let the chicken cool.

Chop the chicken into bite-sized pieces. Place in a mixing bowl with the remaining salad ingredients. In a small bowl, whisk together the dressing ingredients. Pour the dressing over the salad and toss. Place two lettuce leaves on each of three plates and mound the salad on the leaves.

Serves 3.

CALORIES 166, TOTAL FAT 2G, SATURATED FAT <1G, % CALORIES FROM FAT 12, CARBOHYDRATES 24G, PROTEIN 13G, CHOLESTEROL 28MG, SODIUM 85MG

Tuna Tabouleh Salad

TIMER: Bulgar wheat—30 minutes, Ahi tuna—4 minutes

For a perfect summer evening meal, chill this salad for up to one hour before serving. Add some pita chips and fresh greens and dinner is ready!

- ½ pound ahi tuna steak
- 1 cup bulgur wheat
- 2 cups water or low-sodium vegetable broth
- 1 cup cherry tomatoes, halved
- 1 medium cucumber, peeled and diced
- 3 green onions, sliced
- ¼ cup Italian flat-leaf parsley, minced
- 2 tablespoons mint leaves, minced

Lemon Vinaigrette:
- ¼ cup fresh lemon juice
- 2 tablespoons extra-virgin olive oil
- 2 tablespoons water
- ½ teaspoon kosher salt
- ½ teaspoon freshly ground black pepper

Place the tuna in the Side Steamer Bowl and set the timer for 4 minutes. Place the bulgur wheat in the Cooking Bowl and add the water. Place in the Center Steamer Bowl and set the timer for 30 minutes. Start the Steamer. When the timer goes off, check the tuna. The fish will be rare. If desired, continue steaming for up to 4 minutes. When done to your preference, carefully remove the wheat and the tuna and cool slightly.

Cut the cooled tuna into bite-sized pieces. Place the vinaigrette ingredients in a small bowl and whisk to combine. Set aside. In a serving bowl, combine the tuna, bulgur wheat, tomatoes, cucumber, onions, parsley and mint leaves. Dress with the vinaigrette. Serve or chill for up to one hour.

Serves 4.

CALORIES 331, TOTAL FAT 8G, SATURATED FAT 1G, % CALORIES FROM FAT 23, CARBOHYDRATES 45G, PROTEIN 20G, CHOLESTEROL 26MG, SODIUM 267MG

Zorba the Greek Chicken Salad

TIMER: Chicken–18 minutes

Don't argue with the great Zorba. He says...this salad is well worth the time spent chopping and mixing.

- 1 boneless, skinless chicken breast
- 1 clove garlic, minced
- 1 teaspoon dried oregano
- 1 medium ripe tomato, cut into chunks
- 1 medium cucumber, cut into chunks
- ¼ medium red onion, cut into chunks
- 8 kalamata olives, pitted and chopped
- ½ cup fat-free feta cheese
- 8 baby spinach leaves

Vinaigrette Ingredients:
- 1 tablespoon extra-virgin olive oil
- 1 tablespoon water
- 1 tablespoon red wine vinegar
- ¼ teaspoon dried oregano
- pinch kosher salt
- pinch freshly ground black pepper

Season the chicken breast with the garlic and dried oregano. Place in the Side or Center Steamer Bowl and set the timer for 18 minutes. When the timer goes off, check the chicken with the tip of a knife and continue steaming if necessary, until no pink remains and the internal temperature of the chicken reaches 180°F. Remove the chicken from the steamer and cool.

Place the vinaigrette ingredients in a small bowl and whisk to combine. Set aside. Chop the chicken into bite-sized pieces. Combine with the tomato, cucumber, red onion, olives and feta cheese. Dress with the vinaigrette and toss lightly. To serve, divide the spinach equally on two plates and spoon the salad over each.

Serves 2.

CALORIES 254, TOTAL FAT 14G, SATURATED FAT <1G, % CALORIES FROM FAT 47, CARBOHYDRATES 17G, PROTEIN 18G, CHOLESTEROL 23MG, SODIUM 707MG

Lemony Shrimp & Snow Pea Salad

TIMER: Shrimp–8 minutes, Snow peas–12 minutes

Any time I see the words, "lemony" and "shrimp" together, I know we have a winner! This salad is a crowd-pleaser and makes a perfect luncheon entrée.

- 1 tablespoon fresh ginger, minced
- 1 clove garlic, minced
- 1 teaspoon lemon zest
- ¼ teaspoon freshly ground black pepper
- 1 pound medium shrimp, peeled and deveined
- ½ pound snow peas, trimmed
- 2 stalks celery, thinly sliced
- 1 8 ounce can sliced water chestnuts, drained
- ½ cup carrot, grated

Dressing Ingredients:
- 2 tablespoons fresh lemon juice
- ¼ cup nonfat mayonnaise
- pinch kosher salt
- ¼ teaspoon freshly ground black pepper

Place the ginger, garlic, lemon zest and black pepper in a medium bowl and add the shrimp. Remove the seasoned shrimp and place in a Side Steamer Bowl. Set the timer for 8 minutes. Place the snow peas in the other Side Steamer Bowl and set the timer for 12 minutes. Start the steamer. When the timer goes off, remove the shrimp and snow peas.

Plunge the snow peas into a small bowl of ice water. (This stops the steaming process and retains the color of the peas.) Drain the peas. Place the dressing ingredients in a small bowl and whisk to combine. Set aside. In a serving bowl, combine the snow peas, shrimp, celery, water chestnuts and grated carrot. Toss lightly with the dressing and serve.

Serves 6.

CALORIES 130, TOTAL FAT 2G, SATURATED FAT <1G, % CALORIES FROM FAT 10, CARBOHYDRATES 12G, PROTEIN 17G, CHOLESTEROL 115MG, SODIUM 254MG

Godfather Tomato, Mozzarella Cheese & Fresh Basil Salad

TIMER: Rice—60 minutes

Don't mess with success! Fresh basil with mozzarella cheese, tomatoes and green onions are a winning combination for any lover of Italian food.

- 1 cup brown rice (not quick-cooking or instant)
- 1¼ cups water
- 1 large ripe tomato, diced
- 1 cup fresh basil leaves, chopped
- 3 green onions, thinly sliced
- 1 cup lowfat mozzarella cheese, cut into small cubes

Vinaigrette Ingredients:
- 2 tablespoons extra-virgin olive oil
- 2 tablespoons lemon juice
- 1 tablespoon honey
- 1 teaspoon freshly ground black pepper
- ¼ teaspoon kosher salt

Place the rice in the Cooking Bowl and add the water. Set the timer for 60 minutes. When done, remove the rice and place in a serving bowl. Place the vinaigrette ingredients in a small bowl and whisk to combine. Set aside.

In a serving bowl, combine the rice, tomato, basil, onions and mozzarella cheese. Drizzle with the dressing and sing "O Solé Mio" as you toss the ingredients lightly to combine.

Serves 4.

CALORIES 266, TOTAL FAT 9G, SATURATED FAT <1G, % CALORIES FROM FAT 28, CARBOHYDRATES 44G, PROTEIN 5G, CHOLESTEROL 0MG, SODIUM 127MG

Santa Fe Chicken Salad
or Sandwich or Burrito & Beyond

TIMER: Chicken–18 minutes, Corn–30 minutes

This salad is the perfect beginning to wherever you want to go. Spoon it onto fresh greens, pack it into pita rounds, stuff it into flour tortillas or toss it over tortilla chips. It works with everything!

Spice Rub Ingredients:
- 1 teaspoon chili powder
- ½ teaspoon sodium-free garlic powder
- ¼ teaspoon ground cumin
- ¼ teaspoon dried oregano
- ¼ teaspoon kosher salt

Salad Ingredients:
- 2 boneless, skinless chicken breasts
- 2 small ears of corn, shucked
- ½ cup canned black beans, drained
- ½ cup prepared roasted red pepper, diced
- 2 green onions, sliced

Vinaigrette Ingredients:
- 2 tablespoons lime juice
- 1 tablespoon extra-virgin olive oil
- 1 teaspoon honey
- ½ teaspoon chili powder
- ¼ teaspoon kosher salt

Combine the spice rub ingredients together in a plastic bag. Place the chicken breasts in the bag and coat with the rub. Seal the bag and refrigerate for at least 2 hours or up to 12 hours. Place the chicken in the Center Steamer Bowl and set the timer for 18 minutes. Place the corn in a Side Steamer Bowl and set the timer for 30 minutes. Start the steamer. When done, check the chicken with the tip of a knife and continue steaming if necessary, until no pink remains and the internal temperature of the chicken reaches 180°F. Remove the chicken and corn and cool. Place the vinaigrette ingredients in a small bowl and whisk. Set aside. Using a knife, remove the kernels from the corn cob. Combine the corn, chicken, beans, pepper and onions in a serving bowl. Dress with the vinaigrette, mixing evenly. Chill or serve immediately.

Serves 4.

CALORIES 142, TOTAL FAT 5G, SATURATED FAT <1G, % CALORIES FROM FAT 27, CARBOHYDRATES 16G, PROTEIN 11G, CHOLESTEROL 21MG, SODIUM 389MG

Get-Your-Greens-Here! Salad

TIMER: Broccoli–12 minutes, Beans/Peas–10 minutes, Asparagus–7 minutes

You can't get any more green than this! I'm talking about broccoli, asparagus, green beans and peas – think green...and enjoy the crisp, citrus-flavored dressing on these green veggies. (P.S. Did I mention this is green?)

- 1 pound broccoli florets
- ½ pound asparagus, woody ends trimmed
- ¼ pound green beans, trimmed
- ¼ pound sugar snap peas, trimmed

Citrus Vinaigrette:
- 2 tablespoons orange juice
- 1 tablespoon extra-virgin olive oil
- 1 teaspoon orange zest
- 1 teaspoon Dijon mustard
- ½ teaspoon freshly ground black pepper
- ¼ teaspoon kosher salt

Place the broccoli in the Center Steamer Bowl and set the timer for 12 minutes. Place the asparagus in a Side Steamer Bowl and set the timer for 7 minutes. Combine the green beans and the sugar snap peas in the remaining Side Steamer Bowl and set the timer for 10 minutes.

Start the steamer. As the vegetables steam, whisk together the vinaigrette ingredients in a small bowl. Remove the vegetables from the Steamer Bowls and place in a serving bowl. Drizzle with the vinaigrette and toss lightly. Chill until ready to serve.

Serves 4.

CALORIES 99, TOTAL FAT 4G, SATURATED FAT <1G, % CALORIES FROM FAT 32, CARBOHYDRATES 14G, PROTEIN 6G, CHOLESTEROL 0MG, SODIUM 186MG

Snacks, Appetizers & Salads   39

French Potato Salad
with Dijon Vinaigrette

TIMER: Potatoes–20 minutes, Green beans–10 minutes

Try this light and easy version of potato salad. The Dijon mustard adds such a bounce to this - you'll never miss that old potato salad again!

- 1 pound new red potatoes, cut into bite-sized pieces
- 1 pound fresh green beans, ends trimmed and cut in half
- ½ medium red onion, chopped
- 1 tablespoon fresh Italian flat leaf parsley, minced

Vinaigrette Ingredients:
- 1 tablespoon water
- 2 teaspoons extra-virgin olive oil
- 1 tablespoon red wine vinegar
- 2 teaspoons Dijon mustard
- ½ teaspoon artificial sweetener
- ½ teaspoon kosher salt
- ½ teaspoon freshly ground black pepper

Place the new potatoes in a Side Steamer Bowl and set the timer for 20 minutes. Place the green beans in the Center Steamer Bowl and set the timer for 10 minutes. Start the steamer. When done, remove the potatoes and green beans from the steamer bowls and place on a serving platter or in a serving bowl.

Place the vinaigrette ingredients in a small bowl and whisk to combine. Set aside. Combine the still-warm potatoes and green beans with the red onion and parsley. Dress with the vinaigrette and serve. Serves 6.

CALORIES 89, TOTAL FAT 2G, SATURATED FAT 0G, % CALORIES FROM FAT 19, CARBOHYDRATES 12G, PROTEIN 3G, CHOLESTEROL 0MG, SODIUM 203MG

4 chapter four

Side Dishes & Vegetables
Flavorful Rice, Potatoes & Vegetables

Side Dishes & Vegetables 41

Mexican Garlic Rice

TIMER: Rice–45 minutes

Ay Yi Yi! This is so easy to steam!

- 1 cup long grain white rice
- 1¼ cups low-sodium chicken or vegetable broth
- ½ cup canned diced green chiles
- 2 cloves garlic, minced
- ½ medium yellow onion, diced
- ½ teaspoon cayenne pepper
- ¼ teaspoon kosher salt
- ¼ teaspoon freshly ground black pepper

Combine all of the ingredients in the Cooking Bowl and place in the Center Steamer Bowl. Set the timer for 45 minutes and start the steamer. Fluff with a fork and serve.

Serves 4.

CALORIES 188, TOTAL FAT <1G, SATURATED FAT <1G, % CALORIES FROM FAT 2, CARBOHYDRATES 41G, PROTEIN 4G, CHOLESTEROL 0MG, SODIUM 288MG

Spanish Red Rice

TIMER: Rice–45 minutes

Don't let the sweet ground paprika scare you away from this zesty rice! Look for it in the spice aisle of your grocery store. (Okay, if you absolutely have to, you can use regular ground paprika instead, but don't tell anybody I told you. This is just our little secret.)

- 1 cup long grain white rice
- 1¼ cups low-sodium chicken or vegetable broth
- ¼ cup ripe red tomatoes, chopped, with juice
- ½ teaspoon sweet ground paprika
- 2 tablespoons green bell pepper, diced
- 1 clove garlic, minced
- ¼ teaspoon kosher salt
- ¼ teaspoon freshly ground black pepper
- 1 tablespoon white onion, minced
- ¼ teaspoon chili powder

Combine all of the ingredients in the Cooking Bowl and place in the Center Steamer Bowl. Set the timer for 45 minutes and start the steamer. When done, remove the rice from the steamer. Fluff with a fork and serve.

Serves 4.

CALORIES 179, TOTAL FAT <1G, SATURATED FAT <1G, % CALORIES FROM FAT 2, CARBOHYDRATES 39G, PROTEIN 4G, CHOLESTEROL 0MG, SODIUM 123MG

Spice-Rubbed Country Corn

TIMER: Corn—30 minutes

This recipe for corn on the cob is so easy, you could make it in your sleep. Even better, the flavors in this corn are actually so good that you won't need to reach for the butter!

- 4 small ears of corn, cleaned and shucked
- 4 sprays nonfat buttery spray
- 1 teaspoon sodium-free garlic seasoning
- 2 green chives, minced

Spray each ear of corn with one pump of the butter spray. Dust each of the ears of corn equally with the garlic seasoning. Place in the Center Steamer Bowl and set the timer for 30 minutes. Start the steamer. Just before serving, scatter the chives over each ear of corn and serve.

Serves 4.

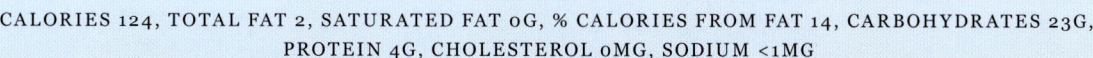

CALORIES 124, TOTAL FAT 2, SATURATED FAT 0G, % CALORIES FROM FAT 14, CARBOHYDRATES 23G, PROTEIN 4G, CHOLESTEROL 0MG, SODIUM <1MG

Zucchini Soufflé
in Red Pepper Shells

TIMER: Stuffed Peppers—20 minutes

This recipe is a special favorite of mine – the soufflé is light and full of onion and zucchini flavors. Make this as a side dish or light entrée.

- ¾ cup egg substitute
- ¼ cup fresh zucchini, chopped finely
- ¼ cup yellow onion, chopped finely
- 2 tablespoons seasoned bread crumbs
- 2 tablespoons lowfat Parmesan cheese, grated
- ½ teaspoon salt
- ¼ teaspoon freshly ground black pepper
- 1 large fresh red pepper, cored, seeded and halved lengthwise

In a medium bowl, mix together with a fork the egg substitute, zucchini, onion, bread crumbs, Parmesan cheese, salt and pepper. Evenly divide the mixture between the 2 pepper shells.

Place the filled pepper shells in the Center Steamer Bowl and set the timer for 20 minutes. Start the steamer. When done, carefully remove the peppers with a slotted spoon and serve.

Serves 2.

CALORIES 182, TOTAL FAT 5G, SATURATED FAT 2G, % CALORIES FROM FAT 23, CARBOHYDRATES 18G, PROTEIN 16G, CHOLESTEROL 6MG, SODIUM 591MG

Pesto & Parmesan Corn-on-the-Cob

TIMER: Corn–30 minutes

Amazing what fresh herbs and cheese can do for corn on the cob! You'll taste a lively pesto flavor (without the fat) in every bite of this delicious corn.

- ¼ cup fresh basil leaves, chopped
- 1 tablespoon Parmesan cheese, freshly grated
- 1 teaspoon extra-virgin olive oil
- 1 tablespoon water
- 4 small ears of corn, cleaned and shucked

Place the basil leaves, Parmesan cheese, olive oil, and water in a blender or food processor and blend until smooth. Using a pastry brush, brush the pesto over the ears of corn.

Place the corn in the Center Steamer Bowl and set the timer for 30 minutes. Start the steamer. When done, remove the corn from the steamer and serve.

Serves 4.

CALORIES 138, TOTAL FAT 4G, SATURATED FAT <1G, % CALORIES FROM FAT 24, CARBOHYDRATES 22G, PROTEIN 5G, CHOLESTEROL <1MG, SODIUM 28MG

Basmati Rice with Cinnamon

TIMER: Rice-45 minutes

Basmati rice is perfect with poultry, particularly when it is steamed with East Indian spices, as in this recipe. The smell of cardamom, cinnamon and cloves will send a delicious aroma through your kitchen!

- 1 cup basmati rice
- 1¼ cups water or low-sodium vegetable broth
- 1 1-inch piece of whole cinnamon
- 2 green pods of cardamom
- 2 whole cloves
- 1 tablespoon cumin seed
- ¼ teaspoon salt

Combine all of the ingredients in the Cooking Bowl and place in the Center Steamer Bowl. Set the timer for 45 minutes and start the steamer.

When done, remove the cinnamon stick, cardamom pods and cloves and discard the spices.

Serves 4.

CALORIES 191, TOTAL FAT <1G, SATURATED FAT <1G, % CALORIES FROM FAT 2, CARBOHYDRATES 40G, PROTEIN 3G, CHOLESTEROL 0MG, SODIUM 150MG

Couscous
with Mixed Winter Vegetables

TIMER: Couscous—20 minutes

Use regular couscous, not instant, to get the best flavor and texture from this small pasta. You can team couscous with just about any vegetable to make a spectacular side dish.

- 1 cup couscous
- 1 cup low-sodium chicken or vegetable broth
- 1 medium carrot, peeled and diced
- ½ medium yellow onion, peeled and diced
- ½ medium red pepper, sliced into strips
- 1 stalk celery, thinly sliced
- ¼ teaspoon salt
- ¼ teaspoon freshly ground black pepper

Combine all of the ingredients in the Cooking Bowl and place in the Center Steamer Bowl. Set the timer for 20 minutes and start the steamer.

When done, carefully remove the couscous from the steamer and serve.

Serves 4.

CALORIES 184, TOTAL FAT <1G, SATURATED FAT <1G, % CALORIES FROM FAT 2, CARBOHYDRATES 38G, PROTEIN 6G, CHOLESTEROL 0MG, SODIUM 170MG

Shanghai Green Beans
with Cashews

TIMER: Green beans–12 minutes

A little bit of fresh ginger and a few cashews change these green beans from ordinary to divine!

- 1 pound fresh green beans, trimmed
- 2 teaspoons fresh ginger, grated
- 2 teaspoons low-sodium soy sauce
- 1 tablespoon cashews, finely chopped, for garnish

Combine the green beans, ginger and soy sauce in a Side Steamer Bowl and toss lightly. Set timer for 12 minutes and start the steamer. When done, garnish with the chopped cashews and serve.

Serves 2.

CALORIES 178, TOTAL FAT 2G, SATURATED FAT <1G, % CALORIES FROM FAT 14, CARBOHYDRATES 23G, PROTEIN 5G, CHOLESTEROL 0MG, SODIUM 177MG

Bok Choy and Broccoli Stir Steam

TIMER: Vegetables—10 minutes

You've heard of stir-fried? My "stir-steam" method of cooking fresh vegetables is even better for you! This Asian dish is great paired with fresh fish or poultry.

- ½ pound fresh bok choy, cut into 3-inch pieces
- ½ pound broccoli florets
- 6 ounce can water chestnuts, drained, sliced
- 2 tablespoons low-sodium soy sauce
- 1 tablespoon balsamic vinegar
- 1 teaspoon fresh ginger, grated

Combine all of the ingredients in a Side Steamer Bowl. Set the timer for 10 minutes and start the steamer. When done, remove the vegetables from the steamer and place in a serving bowl.

Serves 4.

CALORIES 58, TOTAL FAT <1G, SATURATED FAT <1G, % CALORIES FROM FAT 6, CARBOHYDRATES 13G, PROTEIN 3G, CHOLESTEROL 0MG, SODIUM 331MG

Moroccan Carrots

TIMER: Carrots—20 to 30 minutes

A little touch of sweetness in these carrots results in a divine side dish worthy of any dinner entrée.

- 6 large fresh carrots, peeled and cut into 1-inch pieces
- 1 teaspoon ground cinnamon
- 2 teaspoons balsamic vinegar
- 2 teaspoons honey
- 2 teaspoons fresh lemon juice
- 2 teaspoons extra-virgin olive oil
- ¼ teaspoon kosher salt

Combine the carrots and cinnamon and place in the Center Steamer Bowl. Set the timer for 20 minutes and start the steamer. Meanwhile, whisk together the vinegar, honey, lemon juice, olive oil and salt.

When the timer goes off, check the carrots and continue steaming, if desired. To serve, place the carrots in a serving bowl and drizzle the sauce over the carrots while warm.

Serves 4.

CALORIES 80, TOTAL FAT 3G, SATURATED FAT <1G, % CALORIES FROM FAT 27, CARBOHYDRATES 15G, PROTEIN 1G, CHOLESTEROL 0MG, SODIUM 155MG

Brown Rice & Vegetable Pilaf

TIMER: Rice/Vegetables—60 minutes

I like the way brown rice tastes when it's perfectly steamed! It's very mild and works perfectly with the red peppers and peas in this dish.

- 1 cup medium-grain brown rice
- 1¼ cups low-sodium chicken or vegetable broth
- 1 clove garlic, minced
- ¼ cup white onion, diced
- 2 tablespoons red bell pepper, minced
- ¼ cup frozen peas (no need to defrost)
- ¼ teaspoon kosher salt
- ½ teaspoon freshly ground black pepper

Combine all of the ingredients in the Cooking Bowl and place in the Center Steamer Bowl.

Set the timer for 60 minutes and start the steamer. When done, remove the pilaf from the steamer and serve.

Serves 4.

CALORIES 189, TOTAL FAT 1G, SATURATED FAT <1G, % CALORIES FROM FAT 6, CARBOHYDRATES 39G, PROTEIN 4G, CHOLESTEROL 0MG, SODIUM 130MG

Herbed Red Jacket Potatoes

TIMER: Potatoes—45 minutes

One of the best features of red potatoes is that they don't have to be peeled. Talk about easy!

- ½ teaspoon dried parsley
- ½ teaspoon dried rosemary
- ½ teaspoon dried oregano
- 1½ pounds red potatoes, cleaned and cut into bite-sized pieces
- 1 tablespoon fresh Italian parsley, finely chopped
- 1 tablespoon fresh rosemary, chopped
- 1 tablespoon fresh oregano, chopped
- ½ teaspoon kosher salt

Place the dried parsley, rosemary and oregano in the Flavor Tray. In a large bowl, combine the remaining ingredients and toss lightly.

Spoon the herbed potatoes into the Center Steamer Bowl and set the timer for 45 minutes. Start the steamer. When done, remove from the steamer and serve while hot. No butter needed!

Serves 4.

CALORIES 51, TOTAL FAT <1G, SATURATED FAT <1G, % CALORIES FROM FAT 1, CARBOHYDRATES 10G, PROTEIN 3G, CHOLESTEROL 0MG, SODIUM 248MG

Garlicky New Potatoes

TIMER: Potatoes—45 minutes

If you want to keep those pesky vampires away, this recipe is for you!

- 1½ pounds new red potatoes, cleaned and cut into bite-sized pieces
- 3 cloves garlic, minced
- 1 tablespoon low-sodium garlic seasoning
- ½ teaspoon kosher salt
- 1 teaspoon fresh parsley, chopped, for garnish

Combine all of the ingredients except the parsley in a large bowl and stir lightly. Place the potatoes in the Center Steamer Bowl. Set the timer for 45 minutes and start the steamer.

When done, remove the potatoes and place in a serving bowl. Garnish with the parsley and toss lightly.

Serves 4.

CALORIES 59, TOTAL FAT <1G, SATURATED FAT <1G, % CALORIES FROM FAT 1, CARBOHYDRATES 12G, PROTEIN 4G, CHOLESTEROL 0MG, SODIUM 249MG

Super Easy Eggs Benedict w/Hollandaise Sauce - p. 7

Southwestern Style Eggs with Buttered Parsley Potatoes - p. 13

Chinese Shrimp & Water Chestnut Dumplings - p. 27

Vegetable Cream Cheese Pinwheels - p. 28

Salad Niçoise - p. 30

Santa Fe Chicken Salad or Sandwich or Burrito & Beyond - p. 37

Mandarin Orange Chicken with Cashew Broccoli - p. 82

Lemon Dill Salmon with Asparagus & Potatoes - p. 104

Orange Spiced Beets with Walnuts & Feta Cheese - p. 79

Chile Oil Pork Sirloin with Szechuan Vegetables - p. 98

Pesto & Parmesan Corn on the Cob - p. 45

Stuff It! Peppers - p. 92

Tandoori Chicken & Candied Carrots - p. 86

Warm Spiced Apple Crisp - p. 122

Easy Lemon Cheesecake with Mango & Pineapple - p. 117

Gingered Poached Pears - p. 119

Dark Chocolate Custard - p. 116

Sugar Snap Peas & Carrots

TIMER: Vegetables—15 minutes

I like the sound of "sugar snap peas," don't you? The name tells you what's coming and this recipe doesn't disappoint!

- ½ pound sugar snap peas, trimmed
- 1 pound carrots, cut into thin slices
- 1 tablespoon fresh mint, finely chopped
- 3 sprays nonfat butter-flavored spray

Combine the peas, carrots and mint and place in the Center Steamer Bowl. Set the timer for 15 minutes and start the steamer.

When done, place the peas and carrots on a serving platter and spray with the butter-flavored spray.

Serves 6.

CALORIES 49, TOTAL FAT <1G, SATURATED FAT <1G, % CALORIES FROM FAT 3, CARBOHYDRATES 11G, PROTEIN 2G, CHOLESTEROL 0MG, SODIUM 27MG

Fresh Asparagus
with Dijon Tarragon Sauce

TIMER: Asparagus—7 minutes

Nothing says "springtime" like tender, steamed asparagus. Don't hesitate to stock up when asparagus is in season and treat yourself to this special recipe whenever you can.

- 1 pound fresh asparagus spears, woody ends trimmed
- 1 tablespoon nonfat mayonnaise
- ½ teaspoon Dijon mustard
- 1 teaspoon lemon juice
- ½ teaspoon fresh tarragon leaves, minced (or ¼ teaspoon crushed dried tarragon)
- pinch white pepper

Place the asparagus spears in a Side Steamer Bowl. Set the timer for 7 minutes and start the steamer. While the asparagus is steaming, whisk together the remaining ingredients to form the sauce.

When done, carefully remove asparagus from the steamer and drizzle the sauce over the asparagus.

Serves 4.

CALORIES 30, TOTAL FAT <1G, SATURATED FAT <1G, % CALORIES FROM FAT 6, CARBOHYDRATES 6G, PROTEIN 3G, CHOLESTEROL 0MG, SODIUM 47MG

Balsamic Glazed Asparagus

TIMER: Asparagus–7 minutes

With a few added ingredients like aged balsamic vinegar and pimento, a simple asparagus dish is made particularly savory.

- 1 pound asparagus spears, trimmed
- 1 tablespoon aged balsamic vinegar
- 1 teaspoon extra-virgin olive oil
- 2 tablespoons pimento, chopped

Place the asparagus spears in a Side Steamer Bowl. Set the timer for 7 minutes and start the steamer. While the asparagus is steaming, whisk together the remaining ingredients.

When done, carefully remove the asparagus from the steamer. Place on a serving platter and drizzle the balsamic glaze over the asparagus. Turn each spear to coat them evenly.

Serves 4.

CALORIES 40, TOTAL FAT 1G, SATURATED FAT <1G, % CALORIES FROM FAT 27, CARBOHYDRATES 6G, PROTEIN 3G, CHOLESTEROL 0MG, SODIUM 3MG

Pineapple-Glazed Sweet Potatoes

TIMER: Sweet Potatoes—30 minutes, Glaze—5 minutes

These luscious potatoes with brown sugar and pineapple are perfect partners for turkey or chicken! Heating the glaze helps dissolve the brown sugar into a smooth sauce.

- 1 pound sweet potatoes, peeled and cut-into 1-inch chunks
- ½ cup canned crushed pineapple with juice
- 2 tablespoons orange juice
- 1 teaspoon orange zest
- 1 tablespoon dark brown sugar, packed

Place the sweet potatoes in a Side Steamer Bowl. Set the timer for 30 minutes. Place the pineapple, orange juice, zest and brown sugar in a small heatproof bowl and stir to combine. Place the bowl in a Side Steamer Bowl and set the timer for 5 minutes.

Start the steamer. When the timer goes off, remove the potatoes and place in a serving bowl. Stir the warm glaze and pour over the potatoes. Toss lightly and serve.

Serves 3.

CALORIES 202, TOTAL FAT <1G, SATURATED FAT <1G, % CALORIES FROM FAT 2, CARBOHYDRATES 48G, PROTEIN 3G, CHOLESTEROL 0MG, SODIUM 25MG

Parmesan Brusselss Sprouts

TIMER: Brusselss sprouts—30 minutes

These mini-cabbages first steam until tender-crisp and then get a drizzle of walnut oil. They are dusted with Parmesan cheese for extra flavor and tossed with yellow peppers for color!

½ pound Brussels sprouts, cut into quarters
2 teaspoons walnut oil
1 tablespoon freshly ground Parmesan cheese
½ teaspoon freshly ground black pepper
2 tablespoons yellow bell pepper, minced

Place the Brussels sprouts in a Side Steamer Bowl and set the timer for 30 minutes. When the timer goes off, carefully remove the sprouts and place in a medium serving bowl.

Drizzle the cooked Brussels sprouts with the walnut oil and toss. Dust with the Parmesan and pepper and toss again. Just before serving, scatter the yellow bell pepper over the sprouts and serve.

Serves 2

CALORIES 104, TOTAL FAT 6G, SATURATED FAT <1G, % CALORIES FROM FAT 44, CARBOHYDRATES 11G, PROTEIN 5G, CHOLESTEROL 2MG, SODIUM 75MG

Spaghetti Squash
with Fresh Tomato Sauce

TIMER: Squash–30 minutes, Sauce–6 minutes

Toss out that tired, old pasta and replace it with fresh spaghetti squash!

- ½ spaghetti squash, seeds removed
- ¼ teaspoon kosher salt
- ¼ teaspoon freshly ground black pepper

Sauce Ingredients:
- 1 large ripe tomato, diced
- ¼ cup fresh basil leaves, chopped
- 1 tablespoon capers
- 1 clove garlic, minced
- 1 teaspoon extra-virgin olive oil
- ½ teaspoon freshly ground black pepper

Season the flesh of the spaghetti squash with the salt and pepper. Place in a Side Steamer Bowl, skin side up, flesh side down, and set the timer for 30 minutes. Combine the tomato, basil leaves, capers, garlic, oil and pepper in the Cooking Bowl. Place in the Center Steamer Bowl and set the timer for 6 minutes. Start the steamer.

When done, remove the squash from the steamer. Using a fork, carefully detach the squash from the skin so that long strings similar to spaghetti noodles are formed. In a medium serving bowl, combine the squash with the warm sauce and toss quickly.

Serves 2.

CALORIES 77, TOTAL FAT 3G, SATURATED FAT <1G, % CALORIES FROM FAT 34, CARBOHYDRATES 12G, PROTEIN 2G, CHOLESTEROL 0MG, SODIUM 418MG

Acorn Squash with Ground Sage

TIMER: Squash–20 minutes

This seems like a holiday dish to me, maybe because I think of turkey and Thanksgiving whenever I think of sage! You can use this simple recipe for any occasion, formal or casual.

- 1 small acorn squash, halved and seeds removed
- ½ teaspoon salt
- ½ teaspoon freshly ground black pepper
- 1 teaspoon ground sage

Season the inside of each half of the squash with the salt, pepper and sage and press down lightly with your fingertips to adhere the seasonings to the squash.

Place the squash halves in the Side Steamer Bowl, skin side up, flesh side down. Set the timer for 20 minutes and start the steamer. Carefully remove the steamed squash and serve.

Serves 2.

CALORIES 89, TOTAL FAT <1G, SATURATED FAT <1G, % CALORIES FROM FAT 2, CARBOHYDRATES 23G, PROTEIN 2G, CHOLESTEROL 0MG, SODIUM 588MG

Lemon Parmesan Spinach

TIMER: Spinach—8 minutes

A little bit of lemon adds a delightful finish to this fresh spinach dish. You can remove the slices of garlic before eating the steamed spinach, if you prefer.

- 1 tablespoon + 1 teaspoon lemon juice
- 6 cups spinach leaves, tough stems removed
- 2 cloves garlic, thinly sliced
- ¼ teaspoon kosher salt
- 2 tablespoons lowfat Parmesan cheese, grated

Place 1 teaspoon of lemon juice in the Flavor Tray. Place the spinach leaves and garlic in a Side Steamer Bowl and set the timer for 8 minutes. Start the steamer.

When done, remove the spinach and garlic from the steamer and place in a serving bowl. Season with the salt and remaining lemon juice. Sprinkle the Parmesan cheese over all, toss quickly and serve.

Serves 3.

CALORIES 31, TOTAL FAT <1G, SATURATED FAT <1G, % CALORIES FROM FAT 22, CARBOHYDRATES 5G, PROTEIN 3G, CHOLESTEROL <1MG, SODIUM 254MG

Artichokes with Lemon Aioli

TIMER: Artichokes—30 minutes

I use nonfat mayonnaise in this recipe to make a light and yummy aioli that shares the flavor while it spares the fat.

- 3 medium artichokes, trimmed
- ¼ cup lemon juice
- ½ cup nonfat mayonnaise
- 1 teaspoon freshly ground black pepper

Place the artichokes in the Center Steamer Bowl, stem side up. Set the timer for 30 minutes and start the steamer. While the artichokes steam, whisk together the lemon juice, mayonnaise and black pepper. Serve the artichokes on individual plates with a dollop of lemon aioli for dipping.

Serves 3.

CALORIES 94, TOTAL FAT <1G, SATURATED FAT <1G, % CALORIES FROM FAT 2, CARBOHYDRATES 21G, PROTEIN 4G, CHOLESTEROL 0MG, SODIUM 441MG

Orange Spiced Beets
with Walnuts & Feta Cheese

TIMER: Beets—35 minutes

Guess what? Contrary to popular belief, beets don't grow in cans! Fresh beets are surprisingly delicious when steamed and here they are garnished with walnuts, feta cheese and parsley. Enjoy!

- 1½ pounds candy cane beets, peeled and sliced (you may use any small beets)
- 1 teaspoon orange juice
- ¼ teaspoon freshly ground black pepper
- 2 tablespoons walnuts, chopped
- ¼ cup fat-free feta cheese, crumbled
- 1 tablespoon fresh flat leaf parsley, finely chopped

Place the beets in a Side Steamer Bowl and set the timer for 35 minutes. Start the steamer. When done, remove the beets from the steamer and place the beets in a flat serving dish.

Add the orange juice, pepper and walnuts and toss lightly to blend the flavors. To serve, scatter the cheese over the top and garnish with parsley.

Serves 4.

CALORIES 108, TOTAL FAT 3G, SATURATED FAT <1G, % CALORIES FROM FAT 20, CARBOHYDRATES 18G, PROTEIN 6G, CHOLESTEROL <1MG, SODIUM 181MG

Confetti Cabbage Slaw

TIMER: Cabbage—15 minutes

This warm coleslaw is the perfect addition to seafood or poultry! You can serve while warm, or chill the slaw in the refrigerator for a few hours before serving.

- ½ head green cabbage, shredded
- 2 cups carrots, shredded
- ¼ small red onion, shredded
- 1 tablespoon rice wine vinegar
- ¼ teaspoon salt
- ¼ teaspoon freshly ground black pepper
- pinch Splenda® sugar substitute

Combine the cabbage and carrots in a Side Steamer Bowl. Set the timer for 15 minutes and start the steamer. When done, remove from the steamer and place in a serving bowl. Add the shredded red onion.

In a small bowl, whisk together the rice vinegar, salt, pepper and sugar substitute. Drizzle the dressing over the vegetables and toss to thoroughly coat the cabbage and carrots. Cover tightly and chill at least 1 hour or up to 3 hours before serving.

Serves 2.

CALORIES 142, TOTAL FAT 1G, SATURATED FAT <1G, % CALORIES FROM FAT 6, CARBOHYDRATES 31G, PROTEIN 6G, CHOLESTEROL 0MG, SODIUM 393MG

5 chapter five

Entrées Poultry, Seafood, Pork & Vegetarian Main Dishes

Mandarin Orange Chicken
with Cashew Broccoli

TIMER: Chicken—18 minutes, Broccoli-12minutes

Combine magnificent flavors and create an incredible dinner! This dish is pure heaven. Mandarin chicken served in Chinese restaurants is always a treat, but it is typically loaded with fat. My recipe has a mere 8 grams of fat per serving!

Chicken Ingredients:
- 2 tablespoons low-sodium soy sauce
- 1 tablespoon honey
- 1 teaspoon toasted sesame oil
- 1 teaspoon orange zest
- 2 tablespoons fresh orange juice
- ½ medium jalapeño pepper, seeded and minced
- 2 boneless, skinless chicken breasts
- ½ cup fresh or canned mandarin oranges, sliced
- 1 green onion, sliced

Broccoli Ingredients:
- ½ pound broccoli florets
- 1 teaspoon low-sodium soy sauce
- 1 tablespoon cashews, chopped

In a self-sealing plastic bag, combine the soy sauce, honey, oil, zest, juice and pepper. Add the chicken and mix to coat. Seal and refrigerate for a least 2 hours or overnight. Discard the marinade and place the chicken in the Side Steamer Bowl. Cover with the orange slices. Set the timer for 18 minutes. Place the broccoli florets in the other Side Steamer Bowl. Drizzle with soy sauce. Set the timer for 12 minutes.

Start the steamer. When done, check the chicken with the tip of a knife and continue steaming if necessary, until no pink remains and the internal temperature of the chicken reaches 180°F. Place the chicken and oranges on two individual plates and garnish with the green onion. Remove the broccoli and place next to the chicken. Garnish with the cashews and serve.

Serves 2.

CALORIES 274, TOTAL FAT 8G, SATURATED FAT 1G, % CALORIES FROM FAT 24, CARBOHYDRATES 32G, PROTEIN 23G, CHOLESTEROL 41MG, SODIUM 816MG

Chipotle Raspberry Chicken

TIMER: Chicken—18 minutes, Marinade—4 minutes

This chicken is fabulous for those days when you are feeling adventurous. You can find chipotle pepper in adobo sauce in the specialty aisle of your grocery store. (C'mon – live a little!)

- 3 tablespoons prepared mesquite barbecue sauce
- 2 tablespoons water
- 1 tablespoon raspberry jam
- 1 chipotle pepper in adobo sauce, minced
- 2 boneless, skinless chicken breasts
- 1 green chive, minced

In a small heatproof bowl, combine the barbecue sauce, water, jam and minced chipotle pepper. Place in the Side Steamer Bowl and set the timer for 4 minutes. When done, remove and cool, stirring occasionally. Place the cooled marinade in a self-sealing plastic bag and add the chicken breasts. Refrigerate for at least 2 hours or overnight. Discard the marinade and place the chicken breasts in the Center Steamer Bowl.

Set the timer for 18 minutes and start the steamer. When the timer goes off, remove the chicken from the steamer. Check the chicken with the tip of a knife and continue steaming if necessary, until no pink remains and the internal temperature of the chicken reaches 180°F. Place the chicken on 2 individual plates and garnish with the chives.

Serves 2.

CALORIES 136, TOTAL FAT 1G, SATURATED FAT <1G, % CALORIES FROM FAT 7, CARBOHYDRATES 13G, PROTEIN 17G, CHOLESTEROL 41MG, SODIUM 374MG

Sloppy Chicken Joes

TIMER: Chicken–18 minutes

Try this on a busy weekday evening – it will become a new family favorite in no time!

- ½ pound boneless, skinless chicken thighs
- ¼ cup prepared barbecue sauce
- ½ teaspoon onion powder
- 2 whole grain hamburger buns

Place the chicken in the Side Steamer Bowl and set the timer to 18 minutes. Start the steamer. When done, check the chicken with the tip of a knife and continue steaming if necessary, until no pink remains and the internal temperature of the chicken reaches 180°F.

Remove the chicken and shred it on a carving board. Place the chicken in a medium bowl and add the barbecue sauce and onion powder. Mix lightly. Spoon the chicken and sauce into the 2 hamburger buns and serve.

Serves 2.

CALORIES 202, TOTAL FAT 6G, SATURATED FAT 1G, % CALORIES FROM FAT 24, CARBOHYDRATES 28G, PROTEIN 12G, CHOLESTEROL 34MG, SODIUM 650MG

Country Mustard & Green Onion Chicken

TIMER: Chicken–18 minutes

Easy, easy, easy! This simple recipe takes only a few minutes to prepare, but offers a hearty taste!

- 1 tablespoon grainy country mustard
- 1 green onion, minced
- 2 boneless, skinless chicken breasts
- 1 teaspoon fresh parsley, minced, for garnish

In a small bowl, mix together the mustard and green onion. Place the chicken breasts in the Center Steamer Bowl and spoon the mustard mix over each piece of chicken. Set the timer for 18 minutes. Start the steamer.

When done, check the chicken with the tip of a knife and continue steaming if necessary, until no pink remains and the internal temperature of the chicken reaches 180°F. Before serving, garnish the chicken with the parsley.

Serves 2.

CALORIES 130, TOTAL FAT 1G, SATURATED FAT 0G, % CALORIES FROM FAT 19, CARBOHYDRATES 0G, PROTEIN 27G, CHOLESTEROL 68MG, SODIUM 161MG

Tandoori Chicken
with Candied Carrots

TIMER: Chicken–18 minutes, Carrots–10 minutes

Add a fruit or green salad to these exotic dishes and dinner is served! The carrots are a cinch to make and they taste so good served with the tandoori chicken – yum!

- ½ cup nonfat plain yogurt
- ⅛ teaspoon saffron threads, crushed and dissolved in 2 tablespoons water
- 1 tablespoon garlic, minced
- 2 teaspoons dried mint, crushed
- ½ teaspoon freshly ground black pepper
- ¼ teaspoon kosher salt
- 2 boneless, skinless chicken breasts
- 1 teaspoon fresh mint leaves, chopped, for garnish

Carrot Ingredients:
- 3 small carrots, peeled and cut into very thin slices
- 1 teaspoon dark brown sugar, packed
- ¼ teaspoon kosher salt

Combine the yogurt, saffron, garlic, mint, pepper and salt in a self-sealing plastic bag. Add the chicken and mix together to coat the chicken with the marinade. Refrigerate for at least 2 hours or overnight. Discard the marinade and place the chicken in a Side Steamer Bowl. Set the timer for 18 minutes. Place the carrots in the Cooking Bowl in the Center Steamer Bowl. Set the timer for 10 minutes. Start the steamer.

When done, check the chicken with the tip of a knife and continue steaming if necessary, until no pink remains and the internal temperature of the chicken reaches 180°F. Remove the chicken and place on 2 plates. Remove the carrots and toss immediately with the brown sugar and salt. To serve, garnish the chicken with the mint and serve the carrots on the side.

Serves 2.

CALORIES 158, TOTAL FAT 1G, SATURATED FAT <1G, % CALORIES FROM FAT 6, CARBOHYDRATES 17G, PROTEIN 20G, CHOLESTEROL 44MG, SODIUM 582MG

Homestyle Paprika Chicken

TIMER: Chicken–18 minutes

Just like your grandmama in Hungary used to make! And if your grandmother didn't make this and you're not Hungarian, you can still love it.

- 1 tablespoon ground Hungarian paprika
- ½ teaspoon cayenne pepper
- ½ teaspoon dried oregano
- ¼ teaspoon kosher salt
- 1 clove garlic, minced
- 2 boneless, skinless chicken breasts
- 1 large ripe tomato, chopped
- 1 large green bell pepper, chopped
- 1 tablespoon nonfat sour cream for garnish
- dash ground Hungarian paprika, for garnish

In a small mixing bowl, combine the paprika, cayenne pepper, oregano, salt and garlic. Spread the spice mixture all over the chicken breasts, patting to adhere the spices to the chicken. Place the tomato and green bell pepper in the Center Steamer Bowl and position the chicken breasts on top of the vegetables. Set the timer for 18 minutes and start the steamer.

When the timer goes off, check the chicken with the tip of a knife and continue steaming if necessary, until no pink remains and the internal temperature of the chicken reaches 180°F. Remove the chicken and vegetables from the steamer and place on 2 individual plates. Garnish each serving with a spoonful of sour cream and dust each with additional paprika, if desired.

Serves 2.

CALORIES 144, TOTAL FAT 2G, SATURATED FAT <1G, % CALORIES FROM FAT 11, CARBOHYDRATES 14G, PROTEIN 19G, CHOLESTEROL 42MG, SODIUM 299MG

Sage-Rubbed Turkey Cutlets
over Apples

TIMER: Turkey Cutlets—16 minutes

We're talking a seriously great recipe here, folks! I can taste this just by reading the ingredients: sage, turkey, cinnamon and apples!

- 1 tablespoon ground sage
- ½ teaspoon kosher salt
- ½ teaspoon freshly ground black pepper
- 6 ounces thin turkey cutlets
- ½ teaspoon ground cinnamon
- 2 large Fuji apples, sliced
- 1 tablespoon lowfat butter-flavored spread

Combine the sage, salt, and pepper and rub all over the turkey cutlets, patting the spices to adhere to the turkey cutlets. In a small bowl, toss the cinnamon with the apple slices. Place the apple slices at the bottom of the Center Steamer Bowl. Dot with the lowfat spread and place the seasoned turkey cutlets on top.

Set the timer for 16 minutes and start the steamer. When the timer goes off, check the turkey with the tip of a knife and continue steaming if necessary, until no pink remains and the internal temperature of the turkey reaches 180°F. To serve, place the turkey cutlets on 2 plates and spoon the cinnamon apples over each cutlet.

Serves 2.

CALORIES 183, TOTAL FAT 4G, SATURATED FAT <1G, % CALORIES FROM FAT 17, CARBOHYDRATES 18G, PROTEIN 21G, CHOLESTEROL 60MG, SODIUM 586MG

Turkey Cabbage Rolls
with Tomato Sauce

TIMER: Cabbage–5 minutes, Cabbage roll–45 minutes, Sauce–8 minutes

Take a little bit of this and add a little bit of that to create this masterpiece. Don't be afraid of this list of ingredients – the end results are so worth it!

- 8 medium cabbage leaves
- ½ pound lean ground turkey
- 1 clove garlic, minced
- ¼ cup carrot, peeled and grated
- 2 green onions, finely sliced
- 2 tablespoons fresh Italian flat leaf parsley, chopped
- 2 tablespoons egg substitute
- 1 tablespoon ketchup
- ½ teaspoon kosher salt
- ½ teaspoon freshly ground black pepper

Sauce Ingredients:

- 1 14½ ounce can crushed tomatoes with juice
- 1 clove garlic, minced
- 1 teaspoon dried Italian seasoning
- ½ teaspoon freshly ground black pepper

Place the cabbage leaves in a Side Steamer Bowl, set the timer for 5 minutes and start the steamer. Check the cabbage and continue steaming if needed, until the leaves are softened and pliable. Remove and cover with a clean towel to keep warm. In a medium mixing bowl, mix the turkey, garlic, carrot, green onions, parsley, egg substitute, ketchup, salt and pepper until just combined. Do not over-mix.

Divide the meat equally onto each cabbage leaf. Fold each leaf like an envelope and place the cabbage rolls, seam side down, in the Side Steamer Bowls. Set the timer for 45 minutes. Mix the sauce ingredients in the Cooking Bowl. Place the bowl in the Center Steamer Bowl and set the timer for 8 minutes. Start the steamer. To serve, place the rolls on 4 plates and spoon the sauce over the rolls. Serves 4.

CALORIES 145, TOTAL FAT 6G, SATURATED FAT 1G, % CALORIES FROM FAT 35, CARBOHYDRATES 12G, PROTEIN 13G, CHOLESTEROL 45MG, SODIUM 628MG

Spicy Chicken Burritos

TIMER: Chicken—18 minutes, Black Beans—10 minutes, Tortillas—5 minutes

You're probably as tempted as I am by those 10 pound burritos in your favorite Mexican restaurant. Those babies probably have about 1,000 calories and 70 grams of fat! Check out this delish burrito instead – you'll be hooked forever.

- ¼ cup spicy tomato-based salsa
- 2 boneless, skinless chicken breasts
- 1 medium yellow onion, peeled and thinly sliced
- 1 medium green bell pepper, cored and sliced
- 1 tablespoon low-sodium dry taco seasoning mix, divided
- 6 8-inch lowfat, whole wheat tortillas
- 1 cup canned black beans, drained
- 1 medium ripe tomato, diced
- ¼ head iceberg lettuce, shredded
- ½ cup lowfat cheddar cheese, shredded

Place the salsa and the chicken in a plastic bag. Refrigerate for at least 2 hours or overnight. Place the onion and pepper in the Side Steamer Bowl and sprinkle a teaspoon of the seasoning mix over the vegetables. Discard the marinade and position the chicken over the vegetables. Sprinkle the remaining seasoning mix over the chicken. Set the timer for 18 minutes. Wrap the tortillas in aluminum foil and place in the Side Steamer Bowl. Set the timer for 5 minutes. Place the beans in the Cooking Bowl and place in the Center Steamer Bowl. Set the timer for 10 minutes. Start the steamer. When done, check the chicken with the tip of a knife and continue steaming if necessary, until no pink remains and the internal temperature of the chicken reaches 180°F. Remove the chicken and chop into bite-sized pieces. To assemble each burrito, place a portion of the chicken, onion, bell pepper, tomato, black beans, lettuce and cheddar cheese in the center of each tortilla. Fold the sides of the tortilla toward the middle, like an envelope.

Serves 6.

CALORIES 165, TOTAL FAT 1G, SATURATED FAT <1G, % CALORIES FROM FAT 6, CARBOHYDRATES 25G, PROTEIN 13G, CHOLESTEROL 15MG, SODIUM 555MG

Kathy's All-American Meatloaf

TIMER: Meatloaf–45 minutes

My good friend, Kathy, has mastered this tender meatloaf – just like Mom used to make!

- 1 pound lean ground beef
- ¼ cup green bell pepper, finely chopped
- ¼ cup yellow onion, chopped
- 2 tablespoons celery, chopped
- 1 egg, beaten (you may use ¼ cup egg substitute)
- 14 saltine crackers, finely crushed
- 2 tablespoons Worcestershire sauce
- 2 tablespoons fresh parsley, chopped
- ½ teaspoon fresh garlic, minced
- ¼ teaspoon salt
- ¼ teaspoon freshly ground black pepper
- ½ cup prepared ketchup
- 2 tablespoons cherry tomatoes, chopped, for garnish

Mix all of the ingredients except the ketchup and cherry tomatoes in a large mixing bowl and shape into loaf. Place the loaf in the Center Steamer Bowl and set the timer for 45 minutes.

When the timer goes off, use a pastry brush to cover the outside of the meatloaf with the ketchup. Set the timer for 2 minutes and continue steaming to heat the ketchup. Carefully remove the meatloaf from the steamer, garnish the top with the cherry tomatoes and serve.

Serves 5.

CALORIES 198, TOTAL FAT 7G, SATURATED FAT 2G, % CALORIES FROM FAT 29, CARBOHYDRATES 14G, PROTEIN 23G, CHOLESTEROL 97MG, SODIUM 677MG

Stuff It! Peppers

TIMER: Peppers—60 minutes, Sauce—10 minutes

I absolutely love stuffed peppers, so this recipe is one of my favorites. When you put together all of these delicious ingredients and stuff them into gorgeous red, green, orange or yellow peppers, the end result is a knock-out dinner!

- ½ pound ground turkey
- 1 clove garlic, minced
- 1 slice whole wheat bread, cut or torn into small pieces
- ¼ medium yellow onion, diced
- 2 tablespoons fresh Italian flat leaf parsley, chopped
- 2 tablespoons egg substitute
- 1 tablespoon ketchup
- ½ teaspoon kosher salt
- ½ teaspoon freshly ground black pepper
- 4 small bell peppers, tops removed, white membrane removed and seeded
- 2 cups prepared low-sodium marinara sauce
- 1 tablespoon asiago cheese, grated, for garnish

In a medium mixing bowl, toss together the turkey, garlic, bread, onion, parsley, egg substitute, ketchup, salt and pepper until just combined. Place one-fourth of the turkey mixture in each bell pepper. Position each stuffed bell pepper standing up in the Center Steamer Bowl and set the timer for 60 minutes.

Pour the marinara sauce in a heatproof bowl and place in a Side Steamer Bowl. Set the timer for 10 minutes and start the steamer. When the timer goes off, carefully remove the peppers using a large spoon and transfer the peppers onto 4 individual plates. Pour the warm sauce over each pepper and sprinkle with the asiago cheese.

Serves 4.

CALORIES 264, TOTAL FAT 12G, SATURATED FAT 3G, % CALORIES FROM FAT 40, CARBOHYDRATES 24G, PROTEIN 15G, CHOLESTEROL 46MG, SODIUM 449MG

Mediterranean Chicken

TIMER: Chicken–18 minutes

If you can't afford to take a leisurely cruise through the Greek islands, try this recipe instead! You'll love the artichoke, sun-dried tomato and kalamata olive flavors that surround this tender chicken.

- 1 clove garlic
- 2 teaspoons fresh thyme, chopped
- 2 teaspoons fresh rosemary, chopped
- ¼ cup kalamata olives, seeded and chopped, divided
- 2 canned artichoke hearts, packed in water
- 4 sun-dried tomatoes
- 1 tablespoon fresh lemon juice
- 2 boneless, skinless chicken breasts
- ¼ cup fat-free feta cheese, for garnish

Place the garlic, thyme, rosemary, half of the olives, artichoke hearts, sun-dried tomatoes and lemon juice in a blender or food processor. Process until smooth. Pour the marinade into a self-sealing plastic bag and add the chicken breasts. Seal and refrigerate for 1 hour. Discard the marinade and remove the chicken. Place the chicken in the Center Steamer Bowl. Set the timer for 18 minutes and start the steamer.

When the timer goes off, check the chicken with the tip of a knife and continue steaming if necessary, until no pink remains and the internal temperature of the chicken reaches 180°F. Remove the chicken and place on two individual plates. Garnish with the feta cheese and remaining chopped olives.

Serves 2.

CALORIES 149, TOTAL FAT 3G, SATURATED FAT <1G, % CALORIES FROM FAT 17, CARBOHYDRATES 9G, PROTEIN 22G, CHOLESTEROL 42MG, SODIUM 492MG

Chicken Piccata

TIMER: Chicken–16 minutes

This restaurant classic is ridiculously easy to make and you can double or even triple this recipe for guests. Wait until you're at the table before squeezing the lemon wedges over each serving. That last splash is a blast of flavor!

- 2 tablespoons lemon juice
- 1 clove garlic, minced
- 2 tablespoons dry white wine
- 2 boneless, skinless chicken breasts, pounded thin
- 2 tablespoons seasoned breadcrumbs
- 2 teaspoons extra-virgin olive oil
- 1 tablespoon capers
- 2 tablespoons fresh Italian flat leaf parsley, minced, divided
- 2 lemon wedges

In a self-sealing plastic bag, combine the lemon juice, garlic, dry white wine and chicken breasts. Refrigerate for 1 hour. Discard the marinade and place the chicken in the Center Steamer Bowl. In a small mixing bowl, combine the breadcrumbs, olive oil, capers and 1 tablespoon of the parsley. Top the chicken breasts with the breadcrumb mixture, patting to adhere the topping to each piece of chicken.

Set the timer for 16 minutes. Start the steamer. When done, check the chicken with the tip of a knife and continue steaming until no pink remains and the internal temperature of the chicken reaches 180°F. To serve, place the chicken on 2 individual plates, sprinkle with the remaining parsley and squeeze a lemon wedge over each serving.

Serves 2.

CALORIES 169, TOTAL FAT 6G, SATURATED FAT <1G, % CALORIES FROM FAT 31, CARBOHYDRATES 8G, PROTEIN 18G, CHOLESTEROL 41MG, SODIUM 376MG

Roasted Red Pepper Pork
with Rosemary Garlic Lentils

TIMER: Lentils–60 minutes, Pork–10 minutes

Ooh la la! You'll find roasted red peppers in jars in the condiment section of your grocery store.

Lentil Ingredients:
- 1 cup lentils, soaked overnight
- 2 cups low-sodium chicken or vegetable broth
- 2 cloves garlic, minced
- 1 teaspoon fresh rosemary leaves, chopped (or ¼ teaspoon dried rosemary)
- 1 bay leaf
- ¼ cup carrot, diced
- ¼ teaspoon salt

Pork Ingredients:
- ½ pound lean boneless pork sirloin or tenderloin medallions, ½-inch thick, trimmed of fat
- 1 teaspoon sodium-free garlic seasoning
- 1 teaspoon sweet ground paprika
- ¼ teaspoon kosher salt
- ½ cup roasted red pepper, cut into strips
- 2 sprigs fresh rosemary, for garnish

Combine the lentils, chicken broth, garlic, rosemary leaves, bay leaf, carrot and salt in the Cooking Bowl and place in the Center Steamer Bowl. Set the timer for 60 minutes. Season the pork with the garlic seasoning, paprika and salt. Place in a Side Steamer Bowl.

Place strips of the roasted red pepper over each medallion. Set the timer for 10 minutes. Start the steamer. When done, remove the pork and place on 2 individual plates. Garnish with the fresh rosemary sprigs. Remove the cooked lentils and serve on the side of the pork.

Serves 2.

CALORIES 532, TOTAL FAT 8G, SATURATED FAT 2G, % CALORIES FROM FAT 13, CARBOHYDRATES 65G, PROTEIN 52G, CHOLESTEROL 71MG, SODIUM 602MG

Lemongrass Pork with Citrus Rice

TIMER: Rice—45 minutes, Pork—10 minutes

Lemongrass is an Asian herb that has become popular in recent years. It has a strong scent of both lemon and wild grass – no surprise there! Look for it in the specialty aisle of your grocery store.

Pork Ingredients:
- 1 stalk lemongrass, minced
- 1 clove garlic, minced
- 1 teaspoon fresh ginger, grated
- 1 tablespoon lemon juice
- ½ pound lean boneless pork sirloin or tenderloin medallions, ½-inch thick, trimmed of fat
- 1 teaspoon fresh parsley, minced, for garnish

Rice Ingredients:
- 1 cup short grain white rice
- 1¼ cups water
- 2 tablespoons fresh lime juice
- ½ cup canned mandarin oranges, drained

Combine the lemongrass, garlic, ginger and lemon juice in a large, self-sealing plastic bag. Add the pork and coat with the marinade. Refrigerate for 1 hour. Discard the marinade and place the pork in a Side Steamer Bowl. Set the timer for 10 minutes. Place the rice and water in the Cooking Bowl and place in the Center Steamer Bowl. Set the timer for 45 minutes.

Start the steamer. When done, remove the rice from the steamer and sprinkle with the lime juice. Remove the pork and check for doneness. Continue steaming, if desired. When done, place on 2 individual plates. Garnish with the parsley. Fluff the rice with a fork, add the oranges and serve with the pork.

Serves 2.

CALORIES 571, TOTAL FAT 7G, SATURATED FAT 2G, % CALORIES FROM FAT 12, CARBOHYDRATES 92G, PROTEIN 31G, CHOLESTEROL 71MG, SODIUM 65MG

Pork with Apricot Mustard Glaze and Almond Couscous

TIMER: Pork–10 minutes, Couscous–15 minutes

There's something about the combination of "tangy" and "sweet" in one bite that makes me want to dance! The tangy mustard and sweet apricot jam in this recipe are perfect dance partners.

Pork Ingredients:
- 1 tablespoon Dijon mustard
- 1 tablespoon apricot jam
- 1 teaspoon low-sodium soy sauce
- 1 teaspoon dried parsley
- ½ pound lean boneless pork sirloin or tenderloin medallions, ½-inch thick, trimmed of fat
- 1 tablespoon green onions, minced, for garnish

Couscous Ingredients:
- 1 cup couscous
- 1 cup low-sodium chicken or vegetable broth
- 1 tablespoon almonds, finely chopped

Place the mustard, jam, soy sauce and parsley in a plastic bag. Add the pork and coat the pork with the marinade. Refrigerate for at least 3 hours or up to overnight. Discard the marinade and place the pork in a Side Steamer Bowl. Set the timer for 10 minutes. Combine the couscous and broth in the Cooking Bowl and place in the Center Steamer Bowl.

Set the timer for 15 minutes. Start the steamer. When done, remove the couscous and add the almonds. Mix lightly and place on 2 plates. Check the pork for doneness and continue steaming, if desired. When done, place the pork on top of the couscous and garnish all with the green onions.

Serves 2.

CALORIES 547, TOTAL FAT 9G, SATURATED FAT 2G, % CALORIES FROM FAT 15, CARBOHYDRATES 75G, PROTEIN 36G, CHOLESTEROL 71MG, SODIUM 336MG

Chile Oil Pork Sirloin
with Szechuan Vegetables

TIMER: Pork–10 minutes, Vegetables–15 minutes

Hang on to your hat and glasses – this is an exciting ride! The spicy flavor of red chile oil makes everything in this recipe come alive. Serve with steamed brown rice or rice noodles for a super-easy complete meal.

Pork Ingredients:
- ½ pound lean boneless pork sirloin, ¼-inch thick, trimmed of fat, thinly sliced
- 2 tablespoons low-sodium soy sauce, divided
- 2 tablespoons ketchup, divided
- 2 tablespoons rice wine vinegar, divided
- 2 teaspoons red chile oil, divided
- 4 cloves garlic, minced, divided
- 1 small onion, peeled and thinly sliced

Szechuan Vegetables:
- ½ pound carrots, peeled and sliced ½-inch thick
- 1 8 ounce can sliced bamboo shoots, drained
- 1 8 ounce can water chestnuts, drained and chopped
- ½ pound snow peas, trimmed
- 2 large red bell peppers, cut into bite-sized pieces

Place the pork in a plastic bag and add one-half of each of the following: soy sauce, ketchup, vinegar, oil and garlic. Add the onion. Mix the ingredients and refrigerate overnight. Discard the marinade and place the pork in a Side Steamer Bowl. Set the timer for 10 minutes. Combine the carrots, bamboo shoots, water chestnuts, peas and peppers and place in the Center Steamer Bowl.

Set the timer for 15 minutes. Start the steamer. Whisk the remaining soy sauce, ketchup, vinegar, oil and garlic. When the vegetables are done, place in a serving bowl and pour the sauce over all. Stir lightly. Remove the pork when it is at least 140°F on a meat thermometer. Add to the vegetables and sauce. Stir again to coat the pork with the sauce and serve. Serves 2.

CALORIES 463, TOTAL FAT 13G, SATURATED FAT 2G, % CALORIES FROM FAT 24, CARBOHYDRATES 58G, PROTEIN 34G, CHOLESTEROL 71MG, SODIUM 850MG

Baja Fish Tacos

TIMER: Fish–15 minutes, Tortillas–3 minutes

Mild, tender steamed fish teams up with shredded cabbage and lime juice! Skip the fried tortillas and spoon the delicate fish into steamed corn tortillas in authentic Mexican fashion.

- 4 tablespoons fresh lime juice, divided
- 1 tablespoon fresh cilantro, chopped
- 1 teaspoon ground cumin
- 1 teaspoon extra-virgin olive oil
- ¼ teaspoon cayenne pepper
- 1 pound firm white fish, such as halibut or cod
- 2 cups green cabbage, shredded
- 8 6-inch corn tortillas

Place 2 tablespoons of the lime juice, cilantro, cumin, olive oil and cayenne pepper in a self-sealing plastic bag. Add the fish and coat thoroughly with the marinade. Refrigerate for 30 minutes. Pour the remaining lime juice in the Flavor Tray. Discard the marinade. Place the fish in the Center Steamer Bowl and set the timer for 15 minutes.

Wrap the corn tortillas in aluminum foil and place in the Side Steamer Bowl. Set the timer for 3 minutes. Start the steamer. When done, remove the fish and tortillas from the steamer and place on a large plate. Cut the fish into bite-sized pieces. To serve, spoon the fish into the warmed tortillas and top each with the shredded cabbage.

Serves 4.

CALORIES 322, TOTAL FAT 10G, SATURATED FAT 1G, % CALORIES FROM FAT 27, CARBOHYDRATES 34G, PROTEIN 26G, CHOLESTEROL 68MG, SODIUM 73MG

Sesame-Glazed Salmon
with Green Beans Almondine

TIMER: Salmon–15 minutes, Green Beans–10 minutes

Steaming is the perfect cooking method for salmon because the fish doesn't lose moisture during the process. The result is flavorful and tender salmon that is moist – WOW! I've teamed the almondine green beans with the salmon in this recipe to add a special touch.

Ingredients for Salmon:
- ½ teaspoon toasted sesame oil
- 1 tablespoon maple syrup
- 1 teaspoon fresh ginger, minced
- 2 tablespoons low-sodium soy sauce
- 4 5 ounce salmon fillets
- 1 green onion, thinly sliced, for garnish

Ingredients for Green Beans:
- 1 pound green beans, trimmed
- 1 tablespoon unsalted almonds, finely chopped
- 2 tablespoons butter-flavored spread, melted
- 1 teaspoon toasted sesame oil

Whisk together the sesame oil, maple syrup, ginger and soy sauce. Pour over the salmon and refrigerate for 1 hour. Discard the marinade. Place the salmon in the Center Steamer Bowl and set the timer for 15 minutes. In a medium mixing bowl, combine the green beans with the almonds, butter-flavored spread and sesame oil. Toss lightly and place in a Side Steamer Bowl. Set the timer for 10 minutes. Start the steamer. When done, place the salmon on 4 individual plates and garnish with the green onions. Serve the green beans on the side.

Serves 4.

CALORIES 300, TOTAL FAT 10G, SATURATED FAT <1G, % CALORIES FROM FAT 26, CARBOHYDRATES 16G, PROTEIN 31G, CHOLESTEROL 75MG, SODIUM 383MG

Peppercorn Salmon
with Red Pepper Rice Pilaf

TIMER: Rice—45 minutes, Salmon—10 minutes

Just saying this recipe title sounds peppy, don't you think? I think that, after eating this delectable duo, you'll feel more peppy, too!

Salmon Ingredients:
- 1 tablespoon lemon juice
- 1 teaspoon extra-virgin olive oil
- ¼ teaspoon kosher salt
- 1 tablespoon peppercorns, crushed
- 2 5 ounce salmon fillets
- 1 large leek, sliced
- 1 bay leaf

Rice Pilaf Ingredients:
- 2 tablespoons roasted red pepper, diced
- 1 clove garlic, minced
- ¼ teaspoon kosher salt
- 1 cup long grain white rice
- 1¼ cups low-sodium chicken broth

In a small bowl, whisk together the lemon juice, olive oil and salt to form a vinaigrette. Set aside. Scatter the crushed peppercorns on top of the salmon and press down with your fingers to adhere the pepper to the salmon. Place the leek and bay leaf in a Side Steamer Bowl. Place the peppercorn-encrusted salmon on top. Set the timer for 10 minutes.

Combine the red pepper, garlic, salt, rice and broth in the Cooking Bowl. Place in the Center Steamer Bowl. Set the timer for 45 minutes. Start the steamer. When done, remove the salmon and leeks and discard the bay leaf. Place the salmon and leeks on 2 plates and drizzle the vinaigrette over each serving. Remove the rice from the steamer and serve with the salmon.

Serves 2.

CALORIES 574, TOTAL FAT 8G, SATURATED FAT 1G, % CALORIES FROM FAT 13, CARBOHYDRATES 86G, PROTEIN 36G, CHOLESTEROL 74MG, SODIUM 581MG

Lemon Halibut
with Julienned Carrots & Zucchini

TIMER: Halibut–15 minutes

You can julienne the carrots and zucchini by cutting them into short matchstick-sized pieces or you can shred them. Serve over steamed brown rice for a nice weekday meal.

- 1 cup carrots, julienned or shredded
- 1 cup zucchini, julienned or shredded
- 1 pound halibut fillets
- 1 tablespoon fresh lemon juice
- 1 teaspoon fresh dill, minced
- ¼ teaspoon kosher salt
- ¼ teaspoon freshly ground black pepper

Place the shredded vegetables in the Center Steamer Bowl. Top with the halibut fillets. Season the fillets with lemon juice, dill, salt and pepper. Set the timer for 15 minutes. Start the steamer.

When done, carefully remove the halibut from the steamer and serve with the vegetables on the side.

Serves 4.

CALORIES 143, TOTAL FAT 3G, SATURATED FAT <1G, % CALORIES FROM FAT 17, CARBOHYDRATES 4G, PROTEIN 24G, CHOLESTEROL 36MG, SODIUM 190MG

Thai-Style Salmon
with Bok Choy and Broccoli

TIMER: Salmon–15 minutes, Bok choy–15 minutes, Broccoli–10 minutes

Bok choy is a member of the cabbage family and is often included in Chinese recipes, where it is referred to as "pak choi" or "white vegetables." Bok choy is popular for the white stalks (like celery without the strings) and green leaves (similar to Romaine lettuce).

- ¼ cup fresh cilantro
- ¼ cup fresh mint leaves
- ½ jalapeño pepper, chopped
- 3 tablespoons fresh lime juice
- 1 tablespoon fresh ginger
- 3 tablespoons low-sodium soy sauce
- 4 5 ounce salmon fillets
- 1 pound baby bok choy, each cut in half lengthwise
- ½ pound broccoli, trimmed and cut into small florets
- 2 tablespoons fresh mint, chopped, for garnish

Place the cilantro, mint, pepper, lime juice, ginger and soy sauce in a self-sealing plastic bag and add the salmon. Mix the marinade with the salmon to thoroughly coat the salmon. Seal and refrigerate for 2 hours. Discard the marinade and place the marinated salmon in the Center Steamer Bowl. Set the timer for 15 minutes. Place the bok choy in a Side Steamer Bowl and set the timer for 15 minutes.

Place the broccoli florets in a Side Steamer Bowl and set the timer for 10 minutes. Start the steamer. When done, remove the broccoli and bok choy and place on 4 individual plates, combining each portion slightly. Remove the salmon and place each piece on top of the vegetables. Garnish the salmon with the mint.

Serves 4.

CALORIES 222, TOTAL FAT 5G, SATURATED FAT <1G, % CALORIES FROM FAT 22, CARBOHYDRATES 12G, PROTEIN 32G, CHOLESTEROL 74MG, SODIUM 617MG

Lemon Dill Salmon
with Asparagus & Potatoes

TIMER: Potatoes–40 minutes, Salmon–10 minutes, Asparagus–7 minutes

This recipe is especially nice after a hard day – like when you've had a root canal or a five-hour meeting and are looking for some comfort food.

- 1 large lemon, thinly sliced
- 2 5 ounce salmon fillets
- 1 tablespoon fresh dill, minced
- ¼ teaspoon kosher salt
- ¼ teaspoon fresh ground black pepper
- ½ pound asparagus spears, woody ends removed
- ½ pound new red potatoes, cut into bite-sized pieces

Sauce Ingredients:
- ¼ cup nonfat plain yogurt
- 1 tablespoon fresh lemon juice
- 1 tablespoon fresh dill, minced

Place the lemon slices on the bottom of the Center Steamer Bowl. Place the salmon fillets on top and sprinkle with the dill. Dust with the salt and pepper. Set the timer for 10 minutes. Place the asparagus in a Side Steamer Bowl and set the timer for 7 minutes. Place the potatoes in the other Side Steamer Bowl and set the timer for 40 minutes. Start the steamer.

While dinner is steaming, combine the yogurt, lemon juice and fresh dill and whisk until smooth. To serve, remove the salmon from the steamer and place on 2 plates. Drizzle the sauce over the salmon. Remove the potatoes and asparagus from the steamer and serve on the side.

Serves 2.

CALORIES 250, TOTAL FAT 5G, SATURATED FAT <1G, % CALORIES FROM FAT 18G CARBOHYDRATES 18G, PROTEIN 35G, CHOLESTEROL 75MG, SODIUM 360MG

Halibut Peperonata

TIMER: Halibut—10 minutes

If you guessed that the word "peperonata" describes a specialty pizza or an Italian opera, you'll need to guess again. Try this tender halibut served with tri-colored peppers to discover the answer!

- 1 cup red bell pepper, sliced
- ½ cup yellow bell pepper, sliced
- ½ cup green bell pepper, sliced
- 2 5 ounce halibut fillets
- 1 teaspoon dried sweet basil
- ¼ teaspoon kosher salt
- ¼ teaspoon fresh ground black pepper
- 1 teaspoon fresh basil, minced, for garnish

Place all of the pepper slices in the Center Steamer Bowl and mix with a fork until the three colors of pepper are well-combined. Place the halibut fillets on top. Season with the dried basil, salt and black pepper.

Steam for 10 minutes. When the timer goes off, remove the halibut and vegetables and place on 2 plates. Garnish the halibut with the fresh basil and serve.

Serves 2.

CALORIES 183, TOTAL FAT 3G, SATURATED FAT <1G, % CALORIES FROM FAT 17, CARBOHYDRATES 6G, PROTEIN 31G, CHOLESTEROL 45MG, SODIUM 314MG

Citrus Steamed Scallops
with Lemon Spinach

TIMER: Scallops—15 minutes, Spinach—8 minutes

Lemon, orange, lemon, orange and then add a little lemon – this inviting combination of sea scallops and fresh baby spinach are generously seasoned with citrus juices.

Scallop Ingredients:
- 2 tablespoons lemon juice
- 2 tablespoons orange juice
- 1 teaspoon lemon zest
- 1 teaspoon orange zest
- 1 clove garlic, minced
- 1 tablespoon dry white wine
- 1 pound sea scallops, shucked

Lemon Spinach Ingredients:
- 3 tablespoons lemon juice, divided
- 4 cups baby spinach leaves
- 1 clove garlic, minced
- ¼ teaspoon kosher salt

Combine the lemon juice, orange juice, lemon zest, orange zest, garlic and wine in the Cooking Bowl. Add the sea scallops and mix together lightly. Place the Cooking Bowl in the Center Steamer Bowl and set the timer for 15 minutes. To prepare the spinach, place 2 tablespoons of the lemon juice in the Flavor Tray.

Place the spinach in a Side Steamer Bowl and toss with the remaining lemon juice, garlic and salt. Set the timer for 8 minutes. Start the steamer. When done, remove the spinach and place on 2 individual plates. Remove the scallops and divide them over the spinach. Spoon any remaining sauce over the scallops and spinach and serve.

Serves 2.

CALORIES 240, TOTAL FAT 2G, SATURATED FAT <1G, % CALORIES FROM FAT 7, CARBOHYDRATES 14G, PROTEIN 40G, CHOLESTEROL 75MG, SODIUM 649MG

Ahi Tuna with Mango Salsa

TIMER: Ahi tuna—3 to 4 minutes

Care to mango, my dear? Take this recipe out on the dance floor—with fresh ahi tuna, lime juice, red onion and, of course, mango—you will be the star of the evening.

- 2   5 ounce ahi tuna steaks
- ¼   teaspoon kosher salt
- ¼   teaspoon freshly ground black pepper
- 1   cup fresh mango, diced
- 2   tablespoons red onion, diced
- ½   jalapeño pepper, seeded and minced
- 1   teaspoon fresh lime juice

Place the tuna in the Center Steamer Bowl and season with the salt and pepper. Steam for 3 minutes. The tuna will be rare. Continue steaming for 1 to 2 additional minutes, according to your preference.

In a medium mixing bowl, combine the mango, red onion, pepper, lime juice and toss lightly. Remove the tuna from the steamer and place on 2 individual plates. Spoon equal portions of the mango salsa over each tuna steak and serve.

Serves 2.

CALORIES 213, TOTAL FAT 2G, SATURATED FAT <1G, % CALORIES FROM FAT 7, CARBOHYDRATES 15G, PROTEIN 34G, CHOLESTEROL 64MG, SODIUM 360MG

Seafood Paella

TIMER: Rice–45 minutes, Mussels/clams–20 minutes, Scallops/shrimp–10 minutes

You could spend 6 hours making this classic Spanish seafood and rice dish in a large paella pan on top of the stove. Or, you can use a prepared Spanish rice mix and my Steam Heat™ Electronic Steamer to steam it in 45 minutes. The choice seems pretty clear to me!

- 1   6.4 ounce package low-sodium Spanish rice mix, with seasoning packet
- ⅔   cups water
- ⅓   cup low-sodium canned diced tomatoes with juice
- ¼   pound large shrimp, peeled and deveined
- ¼   pound sea scallops, shucked
- ¼   pound mussels, cleaned
- ¼   pound baby clams, cleaned
- 2   teaspoons fresh parsley, minced, for garnish

Mix the rice, seasoning packet, water and tomatoes in the Cooking Bowl. Place in the Center Steamer Bowl and set the timer for 45 minutes (note that, when done, the rice will not absorb all of the liquid). Place the shrimp and scallops in a Side Steamer Bowl and set the timer for 10 minutes.

Place the mussels and clams in the remaining Side Steamer Bowl and set the timer for 20 minutes. Start the steamer. When the timer goes off, check the clams and mussels and discard any that are unopened. Put the clams and mussels in a large ceramic or stoneware serving bowl and spoon the rice over the shellfish. Garnish with the parsley and serve.

Serves 4.

CALORIES 199, TOTAL FAT 3G, SATURATED FAT <1G, % CALORIES FROM FAT 14, CARBOHYDRATES 25G, PROTEIN 20G, CHOLESTEROL 70MG, SODIUM 589MG

San Francisco Style Cioppino

TIMER: Mussels/clams–20 minutes, Shrimp–15 minutes

This famous city is known for a myriad of delicious foods like sourdough bread and clam chowder. You can find cioppino in almost any seafood restaurant on the wharf and the spicy red broth combined with shellfish will satisfy your stomach and your soul on a foggy San Francisco night.

- 1 medium tomato, roughly chopped
- ½ medium yellow onion, chopped
- ½ cup chicken broth
- 1 tablespoon anisette liqueur
- ½ cup low-sodium tomato sauce
- ½ teaspoon freshly ground black pepper
- 1 clove garlic, minced
- ¼ pound medium shrimp, peeled and deveined
- ½ pound mussels, cleaned
- ½ pound clams, cleaned
- 1 tablespoon fresh Italian flat leaf parsley, minced, for garnish

Place the tomato, onion, chicken broth, liqueur, tomato sauce, pepper, garlic and shrimp in the Cooking Bowl and place in the Center Steamer Bowl. Set the timer for 15 minutes. Place the mussels and clams in the Side Steamer Bowls and set the timers for 20 minutes. Start the steamer.

Remove the mussels and clams, discarding any that do not open, and place in a large serving bowl. Remove the shrimp and sauce from the steamer and pour over the mussels and clams. Mix lightly with a serving spoon. Garnish with the parsley and serve.

Serves 4.

CALORIES 163, TOTAL FAT 3G, SATURATED FAT <1G, % CALORIES FROM FAT 16, CARBOHYDRATES 11G, PROTEIN 21G, CHOLESTEROL 78MG, SODIUM 375MG

Ratatouille Provençal

TIMER: Eggplant–12 minutes, Tomatoes/zucchini–10 minutes, Onions/pepper–10 minutes

Ratatouille is a French cooking term for "a stewed dish of vegetables." Traditionally, the vegetables are cooked with a variety of herbs and served hot right out of the pan or after it chills for several hours in the refrigerator. In this recipe, the Steam Heat™ Electronic Steamer does all the work for you! Serve hot or cold.

- 1 teaspoon dried sweet basil
- 1 teaspoon dried thyme
- 1 teaspoon dried parsley
- ½ teaspoon kosher salt
- 1 large globe eggplant, peeled and chopped into bite-sized pieces
- 2 large tomatoes, chopped into bite-sized pieces
- 2 medium zucchini, sliced ½-inch thick
- 2 medium red peppers, chopped into bite-sized pieces
- 1 large onion, peeled and chopped into bite-sized pieces

In a small mixing bowl, combine the basil, thyme, parsley and salt. Place the eggplant in the Center Steamer Bowl and sprinkle one-third of the dried herb seasoning on top. Set the timer for 12 minutes. Place the tomatoes and zucchini in a Side Steamer Bowl and sprinkle one-third of the dried herb seasoning on top. Set the timer for 10 minutes.

Place the red pepper and onion in a Side Steamer Bowl and sprinkle the remaining one-third of the dried herb seasoning on top. Set the timer for 10 minutes. Start the steamer. When done, combine all of the vegetables and herbs in a large serving bowl and toss lightly. Serve while hot or chill at least 4 hours before serving cold.

Serves 4.

CALORIES 98, TOTAL FAT <1G, SATURATED FAT <1G, % CALORIES FROM FAT 7, CARBOHYDRATES 21G, PROTEIN 4G, CHOLESTEROL 0MG, SODIUM 252MG

Spinach Stuffed Portobello Mushrooms

TIMER: Mushrooms—15 minutes

Portobello mushrooms are so big that it's really easy to stuff them with whatever is handy in your refrigerator. In this main dish recipe, the spinach, cheese and spices make the mushrooms memorable!

- 1 10 ounce package frozen spinach, defrosted and squeezed dry
- 1 tablespoon onion powder
- 2 tablespoons Parmesan cheese, freshly grated
- 2 tablespoons egg substitute
- ¼ cup fat-free cottage cheese
- ¼ teaspoon ground nutmeg
- ¼ teaspoon kosher salt
- 4 large Portobello mushrooms, stems removed

In a medium mixing bowl, combine the spinach, onion powder, Parmesan cheese, egg substitute, cottage cheese, nutmeg and kosher salt. Place the mushrooms on the bottom of the Center Steamer Bowl, cap-side down.

Spoon one-fourth of the spinach-cheese stuffing into each mushroom. Set the timer for 15 minutes and start the steamer. When done, place one mushroom on each of 4 plates and serve. Serves 4.

CALORIES 56, TOTAL FAT 2G, SATURATED FAT <1G, % CALORIES FROM FAT 22, CARBOHYDRATES 5G, PROTEIN 7G, CHOLESTEROL 2MG, SODIUM 292MG

Black Bean & Cheddar Cheese Wraps

TIMER: Beans–20 minutes, Zucchini/onions–12 minutes, Tortillas–5 minutes

I'm a big fan of beans (cooked without lard) and cheese! This wrap adds a twist with the vegetables and garlic powder. The secret to success with this is to wrap up the stuffings tightly so that you don't end up with a wrap in your lap.

- 2 cups canned black beans, undrained
- 2 medium zucchini, roughly chopped
- 1 medium yellow onion, roughly chopped
- 1 teaspoon garlic powder
- ½ teaspoon freshly ground black pepper
- 1 tablespoon fresh chives, finely chopped
- 4 8-inch lowfat whole wheat tortillas
- ¼ cup lowfat cheddar cheese, shredded

Place the black beans in the Cooking Bowl and place in the Center Steamer Bowl. Set the timer for 20 minutes. Place the zucchini and yellow onion in a medium mixing bowl. Toss with the garlic powder, pepper and chives until evenly coated. Place in a Side Steamer Bowl and set the timer for 12 minutes.

Wrap the tortillas in aluminum foil and place in a Side Steamer Bowl. Set the timer for 5 minutes. Start the steamer. When the timer goes off, assemble the wraps by placing one-fourth each of the beans, zucchini mixture and cheese in each tortilla and fold like an envelope, leaving one end open.

Serves 4.

CALORIES 200, TOTAL FAT 2G, SATURATED FAT <1G, % CALORIES FROM FAT 7, CARBOHYDRATES 35G, PROTEIN 13G, CHOLESTEROL <1MG, SODIUM 639MG

6 chapter six

Desserts
Delectable Delights with Fruit, Chocolate & More

Classic Rice Pudding
with Raisins

TIMER: Rice—55 minutes

Because I was raised in New Orleans, my favorite sweet treat was undoubtedly a beignet from Café du Monde. These days, I look for desserts that will satisfy my sweet tooth without sabotaging my entire day. This old-fashioned dessert is warm and sweet – just the way I like it!

- ½ cup short grain white rice
- 1½ cups lowfat milk
- 2 tablespoons Splenda® white sugar blend for baking
- ½ teaspoon pure vanilla extract
- ¼ cup raisins
- 1 tablespoon walnuts, chopped
- ¼ teaspoon ground cinnamon

Combine all of the ingredients in the Cooking Bowl except the cinnamon and walnuts and place in the Center Steamer Bowl. Set the timer for 55 minutes and start the steamer.

When done, remove the pudding from the steamer and spoon into 2 dessert bowls. To serve, garnish each with the walnuts and cinnamon and serve.

Serves 2.

CALORIES 380, TOTAL FAT 6G, SATURATED FAT 2G, % CALORIES FROM FAT 14, CARBOHYDRATES 71G, PROTEIN 11G, CHOLESTEROL 15MG, SODIUM 97MG

Exotic Spiced Poached Fruit

TIMER: Fruit–45 minutes

In this recipe the mixed fruit is poached with rich spices to create a delectable "fruity-sauce." Spoon into glass dessert dishes and serve with lowfat lemon biscotti, or any other lowfat biscotti of your choice. Dip the biscotti into the fruit sauce – delectable!

- 1 cup white grape juice
- 3 whole cloves
- 3 cardamom pods
- 1 cinnamon stick
- 1 cup dried fruit, such as apricots, prunes, pears, etc.
- 4 lowfat lemon biscotti

Combine the grape juice, cloves, cardamom, cinnamon and dried fruit in the Cooking Bowl and place in the Center Steamer Bowl. Set the timer for 45 minutes and start the steamer.

When done, remove the cinnamon stick and cardamom pods and discard. To serve, spoon the spiced fruit and juice in 4 bowls and serve the biscotti on the side.

Serves 4.

CALORIES 215, TOTAL FAT 1G, SATURATED FAT <1G, % CALORIES FROM FAT 5, CARBOHYDRATES 48G, PROTEIN 4G, CHOLESTEROL 15MG, SODIUM 38MG

Dark Chocolate Custard

TIMER: Custard—45 minutes

Chocolate lovers gather around! This chocolate custard is a winner and will fill all of your chocolate dreams. Serve it with sweet fresh raspberries as the perfect tangy complement to the rich chocolate flavor.

- 4 ounces unsweetened baking chocolate, melted
- ¾ cup Splenda® brown sugar for baking
- 6 ounces evaporated lowfat milk
- 3 eggs, beaten (you may use ¾ cup egg substitute)
- 1 tablespoon unsweetened cocoa powder
- ½ teaspoon pure vanilla extract
- ½ cup fresh raspberries, for garnish

In a medium mixing bowl, combine the melted chocolate and the sugar until well-mixed, and blend with the evaporated milk by whisking together. The mixture should be very smooth. Add the remaining ingredients except the raspberries, as they are listed, whisking with each addition.

Place the batter in the Cooking Bowl and position in the Center Steamer Bowl. Set the timer for 45 minutes and start the steamer. When done, remove the custard from the steamer and spoon into 6 dessert bowls. Top each serving with fresh raspberries and serve.

Serves 6.

CALORIES 289, TOTAL FAT 13G, SATURATED FAT 7G, % CALORIES FROM FAT 29, CARBOHYDRATES 32G, PROTEIN 7G, CHOLESTEROL 111MG, SODIUM 69MG

Easy Lemon Cheesecake
with Mango & Pineapple

TIMER: Cheesecake–10 minutes

Tangy and tart, this cheesecake really satisfies your longing for silky smooth cheesecake. If you are serving this to guests, you can double the recipe and steam the cheesecake in small springform pans to achieve a classic cheesecake shape (see photo on p. 67).

- 3 tablespoons crumbled sugar-free shortbread cookies (about 5 medium), divided
- 1 8 ounce package fat-free cream cheese, softened
- 1 6 ounce carton lowfat lemon yogurt
- 1 tablespoon Splenda® sugar substitute for baking
- 2 tablespoons egg substitute
- ¼ cup fresh mango, finely chopped
- ¼ cup fresh pineapple, finely chopped

Sprinkle 2 tablespoons of the crumbs in the bottom of the Cooking Bowl. In a bowl, blend the cream cheese with the yogurt, Splenda and egg substitute. Beat until the mixture is very smooth. Pour the batter into the Cooking Bowl. Place a piece of foil tightly over the top of the Cooking Bowl. Place in the Center Steamer Bowl and set the timer for 10 minutes. Start the steamer.

Combine the mango and pineapple in a small bowl. When done, remove the cheesecake and let stand for 5 minutes. Refrigerate for at least 2 hours, or preferably overnight. Remove the foil and sprinkle the remaining crumbs over the top of the cheesecake. Cut the cheesecake into 6 wedges and garnish with the fruit. Serves 6.

CALORIES 200, TOTAL FAT 5G, SATURATED FAT 1G, % CALORIES FROM FAT 21, CARBOHYDRATES 24G, PROTEIN 15G, CHOLESTEROL 8MG, SODIUM 376MG

Baked Apples
with Walnut Streusel

TIMER: Apples–15 minutes

Baked apples are a classic dessert that went out of style in the early 1960s. In the past ten years, baked apples started popping up on restaurant dessert menus once again, probably because they are delectable as well as good for you!

- 2 tablespoons walnuts, chopped
- 2 tablespoons quick-cooking oats
- 2 teaspoons ground cinnamon
- 2 tablespoons Splenda® brown sugar for baking
- 2 tablespoons golden raisins
- 1 teaspoon fresh lemon juice
- 1 tablespoon lowfat butter-flavored spread, melted
- 4 small green or yellow baking apples, peeled and sliced
- ¼ cup nonfat whipped topping, for garnish

In a small bowl, combine the walnuts, oats, cinnamon, sugar, raisins, lemon juice and melted spread. Place the apples in the Center Steamer Bowl. Sprinkle the walnut streusel over the apple slices. Set the timer for 15 minutes and start the steamer.

When done, remove the apples from the steamer and place on 4 dessert plates. Garnish each serving with a dollop of nonfat whipped topping.

Serves 4.

CALORIES 159, TOTAL FAT 4G, SATURATED FAT <1G, % CALORIES FROM FAT 20, CARBOHYDRATES 31G, PROTEIN 2G, CHOLESTEROL 0MG, SODIUM 32MG

Gingered Poached Pears

TIMER: Pears—10/10 minutes

This elegant dessert reminds me of movies I used to watch as a child. The dinner guests were always dressed in tuxedos or evening gowns and the women wore massive, sparkling jewels as accessories. They ate things like poached pears on crystal dessert plates. You may want to dress up for this dessert, too!

- 1 2-inch piece fresh ginger, sliced
- 2 star anise (found in the spice aisle at your grocery store)
- 2 2-inch pieces lemon zest
- 2 tablespoons honey
- 2 tablespoons Splenda® brown sugar blend for baking
- 1 cup ruby port wine
- 1 cup water
- 2 large Anjou or Bosc pears, peeled, cored and halved
- 1/3 cup nonfat half-and-half cream

Place the ginger, anise, lemon zest, honey, brown sugar, wine and water in the Cooking Bowl and mix with a spoon to combine. Add the pear halves and spoon the liquid over the pears. Place the Cooking Bowl in the Center Steamer Bowl and set the timer for 10 minutes. Start the steamer. Turn the pears in the liquid and steam for 10 minutes. Check the pears and continue steaming for 5 to 10 minutes if needed, until the pears are very soft.

When done, remove the Cooking Bowl from the steamer. Let stand 10 minutes. Cover the Cooking Bowl with plastic wrap and refrigerate the pears for at least 3 hours before serving. To serve, place the pear halves on 4 dessert plates and spoon the cream over the pears. Serves 4.

CALORIES 225, TOTAL FAT <1G, SATURATED FAT <1G, % CALORIES FROM FAT 3, CARBOHYDRATES 39G, PROTEIN 1G, CHOLESTEROL 1MG, SODIUM 31MG

Classic Cheesecake
with Strawberries

TIMER: Cheesecake—45 minutes

Steaming is the perfect way to cook a cheesecake because you don't have to babysit the cake. It won't over-brown or become dry along the way. The result is a smooth, light cheesecake. Choose fresh strawberries or any other fresh berry and savor every bite!

- ¼ cup graham cracker crumbs
- 1 cup fat-free ricotta
- 8 ounces lowfat cream cheese, softened
- 1 teaspoon pure vanilla extract
- ½ cup Splenda® white sugar for baking
- pinch salt
- ¾ cup egg substitute
- 1 teaspoon fresh lemon juice
- 1 tablespoon cornstarch
- ½ cup fresh strawberries, sliced
- 1 tablespoon graham cracker crumbs

Place the one-fourth cup of graham cracker crumbs on the bottom of the Cooking Bowl, spreading evenly. Using a whisk or hand-mixer, blend the ricotta, cream cheese, vanilla extract, Splenda® sugar, salt, egg substitute, lemon juice and cornstarch for 3 minutes, or until very smooth. Pour the cake batter over the graham cracker crumbs in the Cooking Bowl.

Place in the Center Steamer Bowl and set the timer for 45 minutes. Start the steamer. When the timer goes off, check the cake. If it is not set in the middle, continue steaming for 5-6 minutes. Refrigerate until chilled, at least 3 hours. To serve, scoop from the bowl and place in 4 dessert bowls. Top with the fresh strawberry slices and sprinkle the remaining graham cracker crumbs over each.

Serves 4.

CALORIES 204, TOTAL FAT 1G, SATURATED FAT <1G, % CALORIES FROM FAT 5, CARBOHYDRATES 26G, PROTEIN 20G, CHOLESTEROL 13MG, SODIUM 710MG

Mango Coconut Sticky Rice

TIMER: Rice—40/5 minutes

How did rice become a dessert? Unbeknownst to many, rice has been offered as a dessert in Caribbean countries for many years and the trend is now spreading around the world. Using "lite" coconut milk helps to lower the fat in this delightfully sweet dessert.

- ½ cup jasmine rice
- 1¼ cups lite coconut milk
- ¼ cup Splenda® white sugar for baking
- 1 ripe mango, peeled and finely chopped
- 1 tablespoon fresh mint, minced, for garnish

Place the rice and the coconut milk in the Cooking Bowl and place in the Center Steamer Bowl. Set the timer for 40 minutes and start the steamer. Carefully remove the rice from the steamer and add the sugar and mango. Mix with a spoon until lightly blended.

Place the Cooking Bowl back into the Center Steamer Bowl and steam for 5 minutes. To serve, spoon the rice into 4 dessert bowls and top each serving with fresh mint. Serve at once or chill for up to 30 minutes.

Serves 4.

CALORIES 235, TOTAL FAT 5G, SATURATED FAT 4G, % CALORIES FROM FAT 21, CARBOHYDRATES 41G, PROTEIN 2G, CHOLESTEROL 0MG, SODIUM 16MG

Warm Spiced Apple Crisp

TIMER: Apples—15 minutes, Crisp—6 minutes

You won't believe how good this tastes until you take that first bite! The "crisp" part of this apple crisp is a perfect crunchy-nutty addition to the warm fruit.

- 1 tablespoon fresh lemon juice
- 4 medium Golden Delicious or other baking apples, sliced
- ¼ teaspoon ground cinnamon
- ⅓ cup Grape Nuts™ cereal
- 1 tablespoon lowfat butter-flavored spread
- 1 tablespoon walnuts, chopped

Place the lemon juice in the Flavor Tray. Place the apples in the Side Steamer Bowl. Sprinkle the ground cinnamon over the apples and toss lightly. Set the timer for 15 minutes. Place the cereal, butter-flavored spread and walnuts in the Cooking Bowl. Mix together until the spread is evenly mixed with the cereal and walnuts.

Place in the Center Steamer Bowl and set the timer to 6 minutes. Start the steamer. When done, remove the apples and place in 4 dessert bowls. Remove the crisp topping and spoon equally over each bowl of apples.

Serves 4.

CALORIES 136, TOTAL FAT 3G, SATURATED FAT <1G, % CALORIES FROM FAT 16, CARBOHYDRATES 30G, PROTEIN 2G, CHOLESTEROL 0MG, SODIUM 87MG

7 chapter seven

Basic Food Charts
Cooking Times & Conversion Charts

FOOD	BASIC COOKING TIMES	NOTES
Cornbread	Follow box instructions	
Eggs		
Hard	18 minutes	hard cooked in the shell
Soft	6-8 minutes	soft cooked
Fruit		
Apple	8-12 minutes	peeled and sliced
Pears	8-12 minutes	peeled and sliced
Peaches	8-12 minutes	peeled and sliced
Pork		
Sirloin/Tenderloin	10-15 minutes	¼-inch thick, thinly sliced
Poultry		
Chicken breasts	16-18 minutes	boneless, skinless with internal temperature of 180°F
Turkey cutlets	10-18 minutes	boneless, skinless with internal temperature of 180°F
Fat-reduced hot dogs	5 minutes	
Rice		
Basamati	35-45 minutes	more or less for desired firmness
White	35-45 minutes	more or less for desired firmness
Brown	45-60 minutes	more or less for desired firmness
Seafood		
Ahi tuna	3-10 minutes	depending on size, cook to preference
Baby clams	10 minutes	do not eat unless opened
Halibut	10-15 minutes	depending on size, steam until fish flakes
Mussels	20 minutes	do not eat unless opened
Salmon	10-15 minutes	depending on size, steam until fish flakes
Scallops	10-15 minutes	depending on size and amount
Shrimp	8-10 minutes	depending on size and amount
Tilapia	10-15 minutes	depending on size, steam until fish flakes
Tortillas		
Corn	3 minutes	wrapped in foil
Flour	5 minutes	wrapped in foil
Whole wheat	5 minutes	wrapped in foil
Vegetables		
Artichokes	20-30 minutes	medium
Asparagus	7-12 minutes	woody ends trimmed
Beans, green	10-12 minutes	
Beets	35 minutes	sliced or quartered
Bok choy	10-15 minutes	
Broccoli	10-15 minutes	
Brussels sprouts	30 minutes	quartered
Cabbage	5 minutes	softened whole leaves
Cabbage	10-15 minutes	1-inch pieces
Carrots	10-15 minutes	grated, julienne, thin-sliced
Carrots	20-35 minutes	large chunks, whole

FOOD	BASIC COOKING TIMES	NOTES
Cauliflower	12-20 minutes	florets
Corn, on the cob	30 minutes	
Edamame	5 minutes	
Eggplant	12 minutes	
Mushrooms	7-15 minutes	
Onions	5-15 minutes	
Peas, snow	12 minutes	
Peas, sugar snap	7-15 minutes	
Peppers, red, green, yellow	5 minutes	sliced in strips for dipping
Peppers, red, green, yellow	20 minutes	softened, skins peeling off
Potatoes, new/red	20 minutes	firm, for potato salad
Potatoes, new/red	35-45 minutes	cut into bite-sized pieces
Potatoes, sweet	30 minutes	cut into bite-sized pieces
Squash, acorn	20 minutes	halved
Squash, spaghetti	30 minutes	
Spinach	6-12 minutes	
Zucchini	10-15 minutes	sliced 1-inch

*The Steaming Chart offers variable steaming times.
This is due to the variations of the size, cut and quantities of foods steamed.*

Volume Conversions

VOLUME	US UNITS	UK UNITS	METRIC UNITS
1 teaspoon (US)	1/6 ounce	5/6 teaspoon	4.93ml
1 tablespoon (US)	1/2 ounce	5/6 tablespoon	14.79ml
1 fluid ounce (US)	1 ounce	1.041 ounces	29.57ml
1 cup (US)	8 ounces	5/6 breakfast cup	236.6ml
1 pint (US)	16 ounces	5/6 pint	473.2ml
1 quart (US)	32 ounces	5/6 quart	946.3ml
1 gallon (US)	128 ounces	5/6 gallon	3.785 liter
1 teaspoon (UK)	1.2 teaspoons	0.2083 ounces	6.16ml
1 dessert spoon (UK)	2.4 teaspoons	0.4167 ounces	12.32 ml
1 tablespoon (UK)	1.2 tablespoons	0.625 ounces	18.48ml
1 fluid ounce (UK)	0.96076 ounces	1 ounce	28.4ml
1 pint (UK)	1.2 pints	20 ounces	568ml
1 quart (UK)	1.2 quarts	40 ounces	1.136 liter
1 gallon (UK)	1.2 gallons	160 ounces	4.546 liters

INDEX

Apples, 124
  Baked Apples with Walnut Streusel, 118
  Cinnamon-Spiced Apples with Blueberries & Yogurt, 16
  Sage-Rubbed Turkey Cutlets over Apples, 88
  Warm Spiced Apple Crisp, 122
Artichokes, 124
  Artichokes with Lemon Aioli, 78
  Mediterranean Chicken, 93
Asian Dipping Sauce, 22
Asparagus, 124
  Asparagus & Ricotta Frittata, 9
  Balsamic Glazed Asparagus, 72
  Fresh Asparagus with Dijon Tarragon Sauce, 71
  Get-Your-Greens-Here! Salad, 38
  Lemon Dill Salmon with Asparagus & Potatoes, 104

Bagna Cauda with Vegetables, 24
Baja Fish Tacos, 99
Banana & Walnut Oatmeal, 14
Beans, 124
  Black Bean & Cheddar Cheese Wraps, 112
  Chicken & Black Bean Breakfast Burritos, 10
  Easy Huevos Rancheros, 15
  French Potato Salad with Dijon Vinaigrette, 39
  Get-Your-Greens-Here! Salad, 38
  Green Beans Almondine, 100
  Salad Niçoise, 30
  Santa Fe Chicken Salad, 37
  Shanghai Green Beans with Cashews, 48
  Southwest Bean Dip with Crisp Red Pepper Strips, 23
  Southwestern Style Eggs with Parsley Buttered Red Potatoes, 13
  Spicy Chicken Burritos, 90
  Steamed Edamame, 21
Beef
  Kathy's All-American Meatloaf, 91
Beets, 124
  Orange Spiced Beets with Walnuts & Feta Cheese, 79

Blueberries, Cinnamon-Spiced Apples with Yogurt &, 16
Bok choy, 124
  Bok Choy and Broccoli Stir Steam, 49
  Thai-Style Salmon with Bok Choy and Broccoli, 103
Broccoli
  Bok Choy and Broccoli Stir Steam, 49
  Get-Your-Greens-Here! Salad, 38
  Mandarin Orange Chicken with Cashew Broccoli, 82
  Thai-Style Salmon with Bok Choy and Broccoli, 103
Brussels sprouts, 124
  Parmesan Brussels Sprouts, 74
Burritos
  Chicken & Black Bean Breakfast Burritos, 10
  Spicy Chicken Burritos, 90

Cabbage, 124
  Baja Fish Tacos, 99
  Confetti Cabbage Slaw, 80
  Turkey Cabbage Rolls with Tomato Sauce, 89
California Turkey Cobb Salad, 31
Carrots, 124
  Candied Carrots, 86
  Confetti Cabbage Slaw, 80
  Lemon Halibut with Julienned Carrots & Zucchini, 102
  Moroccan Carrots, 50
  Sugar Snap Peas & Carrots, 70
Cauliflower, 125
Cheesecakes
  Classic Cheesecake with Strawberries, 120
  Easy Lemon Cheesecake with Mango & Pineapple, 117
Chicken, 124
  Chicken & Black Bean Breakfast Burritos, 10
  Chicken Curry Salad, 32
  Chicken Piccata, 94
  Chipotle Raspberry Chicken, 83
  Country Mustard & Green Onion Chicken, 85

Homestyle Paprika Chicken, 87
Mandarin Orange Chicken with Cashew Broccoli, 82
Mediterranean Chicken, 93
Santa Fe Chicken Salad, 37
Sloppy Chicken Joes, 84
Spicy Chicken Burritos, 90
Tandoori Chicken with Candied Carrots, 86
Vineyard Chicken Salad, 29
Zorba the Greek Chicken Salad, 34
Chinese Shrimp & Water Chestnut Dumplings, 27
Chocolate Custard, Dark, 116
Cioppino, San Francisco Style, 109
Citrus fruits. See also individual fruits
  Citrus Rice, 96
  Citrus Steamed Scallops with Lemon Spinach, 106
  Citrus Vinaigrette, 38
Clams, 124
  San Francisco Style Cioppino, 109
  Seafood Paella, 108
Cobb Salad, California Turkey, 31
Confetti Cabbage Slaw, 80
Conversion charts, 125
Cooking times, 124–25
Corn, 125
  Pesto & Parmesan Corn-on-the-Cob, 45
  Santa Fe Chicken Salad, 37
  Southwestern Style Eggs with Parsley Buttered Red Potatoes, 13
  Spice-Rubbed Country Corn, 43
Couscous
  Almond Couscous, 97
  Couscous with Mixed Winter Vegetables, 47
Custard, Dark Chocolate, 116

Desserts, 114–22
Dijon Vinaigrette, 39
Dip, Southwest Bean, with Crisp Red Pepper Strips, 23

Edamame, 125
  Steamed Edamame, 21
Eggplant, 125

Index

Ratatouille Provençal, 110
Eggs or egg substitute, 124
    Asparagus & Ricotta Frittata, 9
    Chicken & Black Bean Breakfast Burritos, 10
    Easy Huevos Rancheros, 15
    Noteworthy Northwest Scramble, 12
    Run-to-the-Office Breakfast Pita, 11
    Sour Cream Deviled Eggs, 25
    Southwestern Style Eggs with Parsley Buttered Red Potatoes, 13
    Super Easy Eggs Benedict with Hollandaise Sauce, 7
    Zucchini Soufflé in Red Pepper Shells, 44

Fish, 124. See also Halibut; Salmon; Tuna
French Potato Salad with Dijon Vinaigrette, 39
Frittata, Asparagus & Ricotta, 9
Fruit. See also individual fruits
    cooking times for, 124
    Exotic Spiced Poached Fruit, 115

Get-Your-Greens-Here! Salad, 38
Godfather Tomato, Mozzarella Cheese & Fresh Basil Salad, 36
Granola, Gingered Peaches with Cottage Cheese &, 17

Halibut, 124
    Baja Fish Tacos, 99
    Halibut Peperonata, 105
    Lemon Halibut with Julienned Carrots & Zucchini, 102
Hollandaise Sauce, 7
Hot dogs, 124

Lemons
    Artichokes with Lemon Aioli, 78
    Citrus Steamed Scallops with Lemon Spinach, 106
    Easy Lemon Cheesecake with Mango & Pineapple, 117
    Lemon Dill Salmon with Asparagus & Potatoes, 104
    Lemon Halibut with Julienned Carrots & Zucchini, 102
    Lemon Parmesan Spinach, 77
    Lemon Vinaigrette, 33
    Lemony Shrimp & Snow Pea Salad, 35
Lentils, Rosemary Garlic, 95

Mandarin oranges
    Citrus Rice, 96
    Mandarin Orange Chicken with Cashew Broccoli, 82
Mangoes
    Ahi Tuna with Mango Salsa, 107
    Easy Lemon Cheesecake with Mango & Pineapple, 117
    Mango Coconut Sticky Rice, 121
Meatloaf, Kathy's All-American, 91
Mediterranean Chicken, 93
Mediterranean Tofu & Tomatoes, 19
Mexican Garlic Rice, 41
Moroccan Carrots, 50
Mushrooms, 125
    Spinach Stuffed Portobello Mushrooms, 111
    Vegetable Cream Cheese Pinwheels, 28
Mussels, 124
    San Francisco Style Cioppino, 109
    Seafood Paella, 108

Oatmeal, Banana & Walnut, 14
Onions, 125
Oranges. See also Mandarin oranges
    Citrus Vinaigrette, 38
    Orange Spiced Beets with Walnuts & Feta Cheese, 79
    Orange-Spiced Pears with Almond Ricotta, 18

Paella, Seafood, 108
Peaches, 124
    Gingered Peaches with Cottage Cheese & Granola, 17
Pears, 124
    Gingered Poached Pears, 119
    Orange-Spiced Pears with Almond Ricotta, 18
Peas, 125
    Get-Your-Greens-Here! Salad, 38
    Lemony Shrimp & Snow Pea Salad, 35
    Sugar Snap Peas & Carrots, 70
Peppers, 125
    Halibut Peperonata, 105
    Ratatouille Provençal, 110
    Red Pepper Rice Pilaf, 101
    Roasted Red Pepper Pork with Rosemary Garlic Lentils, 95
    Santa Fe Chicken Salad, 37
    Southwest Bean Dip with Crisp Red Pepper Strips, 23
    Southwestern Style Eggs with Parsley Buttered Red Potatoes, 13
    Stuff It! Peppers, 92
    Zucchini Soufflé in Red Pepper Shells, 44
Pineapple
    Easy Lemon Cheesecake with Mango & Pineapple, 117
    Pineapple-Glazed Sweet Potatoes, 73
Pita bread
    Mediterranean Tofu & Tomatoes, 19
    Run-to-the-Office Breakfast Pita, 11
Pork, 124
    Chile Oil Pork Sirloin with Szechuan Vegetables, 98
    Lemongrass Pork with Citrus Rice, 96
    Pork with Mustard Glaze and Almond Couscous, 97
    Roasted Red Pepper Pork with Rosemary Garlic Lentils, 95
Porridge, Strawberries & Cream, 8
Potatoes, 125
    French Potato Salad with Dijon Vinaigrette, 39
    Garlicky New Potatoes, 53
    Herbed Red Jacket Potatoes, 52
    Lemon Dill Salmon with Asparagus & Potatoes, 104
    Southwestern Style Eggs with Parsley Buttered Red Potatoes, 13
Potstickers
    Chinese Shrimp & Water Chestnut Dumplings, 27
    Turkey Potstickers, 22
Pudding, Classic Rice, with Raisins, 114

Ratatouille Provençal, 110
Rice, 124
    Basmati Rice with Cinnamon, 46
    Brown Rice & Vegetable Pilaf, 51
    Classic Rice Pudding
      with Raisins, 114
    Godfather Tomato, Mozzarella
      Cheese & Fresh Basil Salad, 36
    Mango Coconut Sticky Rice, 121
    Mexican Garlic Rice, 41
    Red Pepper Rice Pilaf, 101
    Seafood Paella, 108
    Spanish Red Rice, 42
Run-to-the-Office Breakfast Pita, 11

Salads, 29–39, 80
Salmon, 124
    Lemon Dill Salmon with
      Asparagus & Potatoes, 104
    Noteworthy Northwest
      Scramble, 12
    Peppercorn Salmon with Red
      Pepper Rice Pilaf, 101
    Sesame-Glazed Salmon with
      Green Beans Almondine, 100
    Thai-Style Salmon with Bok Choy
      and Broccoli, 103
San Francisco Style Cioppino, 109
Santa Fe Chicken Salad, 37
Sauces
    Asian Dipping Sauce, 22
    Bagna Cauda with
      Vegetables, 24
    Fresh Tomato Sauce, 75
    Hollandaise Sauce, 7
    Tomato Sauce, 89
Scallops, 124
    Citrus Steamed Scallops with
      Lemon Spinach, 106
    Seafood Paella, 108
Seafood. See also individual
  seafood
    cooking times for, 124
    San Francisco Style Cioppino, 109
    Seafood Paella, 108
Shanghai Green Beans with
  Cashews, 48
Shrimp, 124
    Chilled Shrimp with Cocktail
      Sauce, 26
    Chinese Shrimp & Water Chestnut
      Dumplings, 27
    Lemony Shrimp & Snow Pea
      Salad, 35
    San Francisco Style Cioppino, 109
    Seafood Paella, 108
Slaw, Confetti Cabbage, 80
Sloppy Chicken Joes, 84
Southwestern Style Eggs with
  Parsley Buttered Red Potatoes, 13
Spanish Red Rice, 42
Spinach, 125
    Citrus Steamed Scallops with
      Lemon Spinach, 106
    Lemon Parmesan Spinach, 77
    Spinach Stuffed Portobello
      Mushrooms, 111
Squash, 125. See also Zucchini
    Acorn Squash with
      Ground Sage, 76
    Spaghetti Squash with Fresh
      Tomato Sauce, 75
Steam Heat™ Electronic Steamer
    cooking times for, 124–25
    features of, 5
Strawberries
    Classic Cheesecake with
      Strawberries, 120
    Strawberries & Cream Porridge, 8
Stuff It! Peppers, 92
Sweet Potatoes,
  Pineapple-Glazed, 73

Tacos, Baja Fish, 99
Tilapia, 124
Tandoori Chicken with Candied
  Carrots, 86
Thai-Style Salmon with Bok Choy
  and Broccoli, 103
Tofu & Tomatoes,
  Mediterranean, 19
Tomatoes
    California Turkey Cobb Salad, 31
    Fresh Tomato Sauce, 75
    Godfather Tomato, Mozzarella
      Cheese & Fresh Basil Salad, 36
    Mediterranean Tofu &
      Tomatoes, 19
    Ratatouille Provençal, 110
    Salad Niçoise, 30
    Spanish Red Rice, 42
    Tomato Sauce, 89
    Tuna Tabouleh Salad, 33
Tortillas, 124
    Baja Fish Tacos, 99
    Black Bean & Cheddar Cheese
      Wraps, 112
    Chicken & Black Bean Breakfast
      Burritos, 10
    Easy Huevos Rancheros, 15
    Spicy Chicken Burritos, 90
    Vegetable Cream Cheese
      Pinwheels, 28
Tuna, 124
    Ahi Tuna with Mango Salsa, 107
    Salad Niçoise, 30
    Tuna Tabouleh Salad, 33
Turkey, 124
    California Turkey Cobb Salad, 31
    Run-to-the-Office Breakfast
      Pita, 11
    Sage-Rubbed Turkey Cutlets over
      Apples, 88
    Stuff It! Peppers, 92
    Turkey Cabbage Rolls with
      Tomato Sauce, 89
    Turkey Potstickers, 22

Vegetables. See also individual
  vegetables
    Bagna Cauda with
      Vegetables, 24
    Brown Rice & Vegetable Pilaf, 51
    Chile Oil Pork Sirloin with
      Szechuan Vegetables, 98
    cooking times for, 124–25
    Couscous with Mixed Winter
      Vegetables, 47
    Vegetable Cream Cheese
      Pinwheels, 28
Vineyard Chicken Salad, 29

Zorba the Greek Chicken Salad, 34
Zucchini, 125
    Black Bean & Cheddar Cheese
      Wraps, 112
    Lemon Halibut with Julienned
      Carrots & Zucchini, 102
    Ratatouille Provençal, 110
    Zucchini Soufflé in Red Pepper
      Shells, 44